# ROOKIE COACHES SWIMMING GUIDE

**John Leonard**
American Swim Coaches Association

**American Sport Education Program**

**Human Kinetics**

ry of Congress Cataloging-in-Publication Data

e / American Sport Education Program and
John Leonard
    p.   cm.
   ISBN 0-87322-645-3
    1.Swimming for children--Coaching.   I. Leonard, John, 1948- .
  II. American Sport Education Program.
  GV837.65.R66  1995
  797.2'1--dc20              94-27661
                          CIP

ISBN: 0-87322-645-3

**Swimming Consultant:** John Leonard, American Swim Coaches Association; **Developmental Editor:** Jan Colarusso Seeley; **Assistant Editors:** Jacqueline Blakley, Anna Curry, Ed Giles, and Karen Bojda; **Copyeditor:** Molly Bentsen; **Proofreader:** Pam Johnson; **Production Manager:** Kris Slamans; **Typesetter:** Ruby Zimmerman; **Text Designer:** Keith Blomberg; **Layout Artist:** Tara Welsch; **Cover Design:** Jack Davis; **Cover Photo:** Will Zehr; **Interior Art:** Tim Stiles, cartoons; Sharon Barner, line drawings; **Printer:** United Graphics

Human Kinetics books are available at special discounts for bulk purchase. Special editions or book excerpts can also be created to specification. For details, contact the Special Sales Manager at Human Kinetics.

Printed in the United States of America    10  9  8  7  6  5  4  3  2

**Human Kinetics**
P.O. Box 5076, Champaign, IL 61825-5076
1-800-747-4457

*Canada:* Human Kinetics, Box 24040, Windsor, ON N8Y 4Y9
1-800-465-7301 (in Canada only)

*Europe:* Human Kinetics, P.O. Box IW14, Leeds LS16 6TR, United Kingdom
(44) 1132 781708

*Australia:* Human Kinetics, 2 Ingrid Street, Clapham 5062, South Australia
(08) 371 3755

*New Zealand:* Human Kinetics, P.O. Box 105-231, Auckland 1
(09) 523 3462

# Contents

# Welcome to Coaching!

Coaching young swimmers is an exciting way to be involved in swimming. But it isn't easy. Some coaches are overwhelmed by the responsibilities of helping athletes through their early sport experiences. And that's not surprising, because coaching young athletes requires a lot more than just watching swimmers fly off the starting blocks. It involves preparing them physically and mentally to compete effectively, fairly, and safely in swimming while providing them with a positive role model.

This book will help you meet the challenges and experience the rewards of coaching young athletes. We call it the *Rookie Coaches Swimming Guide* because it is intended as a practical resource for adults with little formal training in coaching swimming. In this guide you'll learn how to apply coaching principles and teach fundamental swimming skills and techniques to young swimmers.

The American Sport Education Program (ASEP) thanks John Leonard of the American Swim Coaches Association for contributing his swimming knowledge and expertise to this guide. The combination of a great understanding of swimming with ASEP's expertise in important coaching principles makes the *Rookie Coaches Swimming Guide* a strong starting point for any coach who wants to learn more about coaching swimming.

This book also serves as a text for ASEP's Rookie Coaches Course. If you would like more information about the course, about ASEP, about curriculums for sport administrators and parents of athletes—**SportDirector** and **SportParent**—or about additional resources available for swimming coaches, please contact us at

ASEP
P.O. Box 5076
Champaign, IL 61825-5076
1-800-747-5698

Good coaching!

# Who, Me . . . a Coach?

If you're like most youth league coaches, you were recruited from the ranks of concerned parents, sports enthusiasts, or community volunteers. And, like many rookie *and* veteran coaches, you probably have had little formal instruction in how to coach. But swimming is probably a part of your sport background. You may have been a competitive swimmer in high school or college, worked as a lifeguard, or just took swim lessons as a kid. So when the call went out for coaches to assist with the local youth swimming program, you

answered because you like children, you wanted to get back into the swimming scene, you're community-minded, and maybe you are even interested in starting a coaching career.

## I Want to Help, But . . .

Your initial coaching assignment may be difficult. Like many volunteers, you don't know everything there is to know about swimming or about how to work with children ages 6 to 14. Relax—this *Rookie Coaches*

*Swimming Guide* will help you learn the basics for coaching swimming effectively. In the coming pages you will find the answers to such common questions as the following:

- What tools do I need to be a good coach?
- How can I best communicate with my swimmers?
- How do I go about teaching swimming skills?
- What can I do to promote safety?
- What actions do I take when someone is injured?
- What are the basic rules, skills, and programs for swimming?
- What practice drills will improve my swimmers' skills?

Before answering these questions, let's take a look at what's involved in being a coach.

## Am I a Parent or a Coach?

Many coaches are parents, but the two roles should not be confused. As a parent you are responsible only to yourself and your child; as a coach you are responsible to the organization, all the swimmers on the team (including your child), and their parents. Because of

these additional responsibilities, your behavior at the swimming pool will differ from at home, and your son or daughter may not understand why. Take these steps to avoid problems when coaching your child:

- Ask your child if he or she wants you to coach the team.
- Explain why you want to be involved with the team.
- Discuss with your child your new responsibilities and how they will affect your relationship when you are coaching.
- Limit your "coach" behavior to the times when you are in a coaching role.
- To keep your role clear in your child's mind, avoid parenting during practice or meet situations.
- Reaffirm that you love your child whatever her or his performance in the swimming pool.

## What Are My Responsibilities as a Coach?

A coach assumes the responsibility of doing everything possible to ensure that the youngsters on her or his team will have an enjoyable and safe sporting experience while they learn sport skills. If you're ever in doubt about your approach, remind yourself that "fun and fundamentals" are most important.

### Provide an Enjoyable Experience

Swimming should be fun. Even if nothing else is accomplished, make certain your swimmers have fun. Take the fun out of swimming and you'll take the children out of the sport.

Children enter sport for a number of reasons—to meet and play with other children, to develop physically, to learn skills—but their major objective is to have fun. Help them satisfy this goal by injecting humor and variety into your practices. Make meets nonthreatening, festive experiences for your swimmers. Such an approach will increase

their desire to participate in the future, which should be the primary goal of youth sport.

Unit 2 will help you learn how to satisfy your swimmers' yearning for fun and keep winning in perspective. And Unit 3 will describe how to communicate this perspective effectively.

### Provide a Safe Experience

You are responsible for planning and teaching activities so that the progression between them minimizes risks (see Units 4 and 5). You also must ensure that the facility where your team practices and competes and the equipment that team members use are free of hazards. You must also conduct well-supervised practices. Finally, you need to protect yourself from any legal liability that might arise from your involvement as a coach. Unit 5 will help you take the appropriate precautions.

### Teach Basic Swimming Skills

In becoming a coach, you take on the role of educator. You must teach your young athletes the fundamental skills and strategies necessary for success in swimming. That means you need to "go to school." If you don't

know the basics of swimming now, you can learn them by reading the second half of this guide. And even if you know swimming as an athlete, do you know how to teach it? This book will help you get started.

You'll also find that you are better able to teach the swimming skills and techniques you do know if you plan your practices. Unit 4 provides some guidelines for effective practice planning.

Many valuable swimming books are also available to help you learn, including those offered by Human Kinetics. See the list in the back of this guide, or call 1-800-747-4457 for more information.

## Where Do I Get Help?

Veteran coaches in your league are an especially good source of information and assistance. These coaches have experienced the same emotions and concerns you are facing; their advice and feedback can be invaluable as you work through your first few seasons of coaching.

You can also learn a great deal by observing local high school and college swimming coaches in practices and games. You might even ask a few of the coaches you respect most to lend a hand with a couple of your practices.

You can get additional help by attending swimming clinics, reading swimming publications, and studying instructional videos. Contact the American Sport Education Program or a national swimming organization for more coaching information:

American Swim Coaches Association
301 SE 20th St.
Fort Lauderdale, FL 33316
Phone: 800-356-2722

YMCA Swimming
Laura Slane, Head of Aquatics
101 N. Wacker Dr.
Chicago, IL 60606
Phone: 312-977-0031

National Interscholastic Swimming
   Coaches Association
c/o Walter Olsewski
P.O. Box 1102
Central Islip, NY 11722

College Swimming Coaches Association
   of America
Bob Boettner, Executive Director
2411 N. Oak St., Suite T303
Myrtle Beach, SC 29577
Phone: 803-626-7752

United States Swimming
One Olympic Plaza
1750 E. Boulder St.
Colorado Springs, CO 80909
Phone: 719-578-4578

Coaching swimming is a rewarding experience. And just as you want your swimmers to learn and practice to be the best they can be, learn all you can about coaching so you can be the best swimming coach you can be.

# What Tools Do I Need to Coach?

Have you acquired the traditional coaching tools— things like stopwatches, starting devices, a clipboard, and a video player? They'll help you, to be sure, but to be a successful coach you'll need five other *tools* that cannot be bought. These tools are available only through self-examination and hard work, but they're easy to remember with the acronym *COACH*:

**C** —Comprehension

**O** —Outlook

**A** —Affection

**C** —Character

**H** —Humor

## Comprehension

*Comprehension* of the rules, skills, and techniques of swimming is required. It is essential that you understand the basic elements of the sport. To assist your learning, the second half of this guide describes how swimming meets are conducted and outlines specific swimming techniques. In the swimming-specific section of the guide, you'll also find a variety of drills to use in developing young swimmers' skills. And, perhaps most importantly, you'll learn how to apply your knowledge of the sport in teaching it to your swim team.

To improve your comprehension of swimming, take the following steps:

- Read the sport-specific section of this book.
- Consider reading other books on coaching swimming, including those available from Human Kinetics (see the back of the book to order).
- Contact any of the organizations listed on page 4.
- Attend swim coaching clinics.
- Talk with other, more experienced swim coaches.
- Observe local college, high school, and youth swim meets.
- Watch swim meets on television or on videotape.

In addition to understanding swimming, you must implement proper training and safety methods so your swimmers can par-

ticipate with little risk of injury. Even then, some injuries will occur. And, more often than not, you'll be the first person responding to your athletes' injuries, so be sure you understand the basic emergency care procedures described in Unit 5. Also read in that unit how to handle more serious sport injury situations.

## Outlook

This coaching tool refers to your perspective and goals—what you are seeking as a coach. The most common coaching objectives are to have fun; to help swimmers develop their physical, mental, and social skills; and to win. Thus, *Outlook* involves the priorities you set, your planning, and your vision for the future.

To work successfully with children in a sport setting, you must know your priorities. In what order do you rank the importance of fun, development, and winning?

Answer the following questions to examine your objectives.

*Of which situation would you be most proud?*

a. Knowing that each participant enjoyed competing in swimming.

b. Seeing that all swimmers improved their skills.

c. Winning the league championship.

*Which statement best reflects your thoughts about sport?*

a. If it isn't fun, don't do it.
b. Everyone should learn something every day.
c. Sport isn't fun if you don't win.

*How would you like your swimmers to remember you?*

a. As a coach who was fun to swim for.
b. As a coach who taught good fundamental skills.
c. As a coach who had a winning record.

*Which would you most like to hear a parent of a child on your team say?*

a. Jake really had a good time swimming this year.
b. Carmen learned some important lessons in swimming this year.
c. Darrin competed on the first-place swim team this year.

*Which of the following would be the most rewarding moment of your season?*

a. Having your team not want to stop swimming after practice was over.
b. Seeing your swimmers finally master the skill of proper backstroke starts.
c. Winning the league championship.

Look over your answers. If you most often selected "a" responses, then having fun is most important to you. A majority of "b" answers suggests that skill development is what attracts you to coaching. And if "c" was your most frequent response, winning is tops on your list of coaching priorities.

Most coaches say fun and development are more important, but when actually coaching, some coaches emphasize—indeed over-emphasize—winning. You will also face situations that challenge you to keep winning in its proper perspective. During such moments you'll have to choose between emphasizing your swimmers' development and winning. If your priorities are in order, your swimmers' well-being will take precedence over your team's win-loss record every time.

Take the following actions to better define your outlook:

1. Determine your priorities for the season.
2. Prepare for situations that challenge your priorities.
3. Set goals for yourself and your swimmers that are consistent with those priorities.
4. Plan how you and your swimmers can best attain your goals.
5. Review your goals frequently to be sure you are staying on track.

It is particularly important for coaches to permit all young athletes to participate. Each youngster should have an opportunity to develop skills and have fun—even if it means sacrificing a win or two during the season. After all, wouldn't you prefer losing a couple of meets to losing a couple of swimmers' interest?

Remember that the challenge and joy of sport is experienced through *striving to win*, not through winning itself. A coach who encourages all athletes to compete and develop skills will—in the end—come out on top.

ASEP has a motto that will help you keep your outlook in the best interest of the kids on your team. It summarizes in four words all you need to remember when establishing your coaching priorities:

*Athletes First, Winning Second*

This motto recognizes that striving to win is an important, even vital, part of sport. But it emphatically states that no efforts in striving to win should be made at the expense of athletes' well-being, development, and enjoyment.

## Affection

This is another vital *tool* you will want to have in your coaching kit: a genuine concern for the young people you coach. *Affection* involves having a love for children, a desire to share with them your love and knowledge of sport, and the patience and understanding that allows every child swimming with you to grow from involvement in swimming.

Successful coaches have a real concern for the health and welfare of their athletes. They care that each child on the team has an enjoyable and successful experience. They have a genuine desire to work with children and be involved in their growth. And they have the patience to work with those who are slower to learn or less capable of performing. If you have such qualities or are willing to work hard to develop them, then you have the affection necessary to coach young athletes.

There are many ways to demonstrate your affection and patience, including these:

- Make an effort to get to know each swimmer on your team.
- Treat each swimmer as an individual.
- Empathize with swimmers trying to learn new and difficult skills.
- Treat athletes as you would like to be treated under similar circumstances.
- Remain in control of your emotions.
- Show your enthusiasm for being involved with your team.
- Keep an upbeat and positive tone in all of your communications.

## Character

Youngsters learn by listening to what adults say. But they learn even more by watching the behaviors of certain important individuals. As a coach, you are likely to be a significant figure in the lives of your swimmers. Will you be a good role model?

Having good *Character* means modeling appropriate behaviors for sport and life. That means more than just saying the right things. What you say and what you do must match. There is no place in coaching for the "Do as I say, not as I do" philosophy. Be in control of yourself before, during, and after all meets and practices. And don't be afraid to admit if you are wrong. No one is perfect!

Consider the following steps to being a good role model:

- Take stock of your strengths and weaknesses.
- Build on your strengths.
- Set goals for yourself to improve in any areas you would not like to see mimicked.
- Apologize to your team and to yourself if you slip up. You'll do better next time.

## Humor

*Humor* is often overlooked as a coaching tool. For our use it means having the ability to laugh *at* yourself and *with* your swimmers during practices and meets. Nothing helps balance the tone of a serious skill-learning session like a chuckle or two. And a sense of humor puts in perspective the many mistakes your young swimmers will make. So don't get upset over each miscue or respond negatively to erring athletes. Allow your swimmers and yourself to enjoy the ups, and don't dwell on the downs.

Here are some tips for injecting humor into your practices:

- Make practices fun by including a variety of activities.
- Keep all swimmers involved in drills and progressions.
- Consider laughter from your swimmers a sign of enjoyment, not of a lack of discipline.

- Talk with each person during every practice about something other than the sport of swimming.
- Develop a personal relationship with each of your athletes, perhaps based on a shared sense of humor.
- Smile!

## Where Do You Stand?

To take stock of your "coaching tool kit," use the following form to rank yourself on each of the three questions concerning the five coaching tools. Circle the number that best describes your *present* status on each item. Then total your score for each tool.

| Not at all | | Somewhat | | Very much so |
|---|---|---|---|---|
| 1 | 2 | 3 | 4 | 5 |

*Comprehension*

1. Could you explain the rules of swimming to parents without studying for a long time? — 1 2 3 4 5
2. Do you know how to organize and conduct safe swim practices? — 1 2 3 4 5
3. Do you know how to provide first aid for most common minor sport injuries? — 1 2 3 4 5

*Comprehension score:* ———

*Outlook*

4. Do you keep winning in its proper perspective when you coach? — 1 2 3 4 5
5. Do you plan for every meeting, practice, and swim meet? — 1 2 3 4 5
6. Do you have a vision of what you want your swimmers to be able to do by the end of the season? — 1 2 3 4 5

*Outlook score:* ———

*Affection*

7. Do you enjoy working with children? — 1 2 3 4 5
8. Are you patient with youngsters learning new skills? — 1 2 3 4 5
9. Are you able to show your swimmers that you care? — 1 2 3 4 5

*Affection score:* ———

(continued)

*(continued)*

| Not at all | | Somewhat | | Very much so |
| --- | --- | --- | --- | --- |
| 1 | 2 | 3 | 4 | 5 |

### *Character*

10. Are your words and behaviors consistent?    1 2 3 4 5

11. Are you a good model for your athletes?    1 2 3 4 5

12. Do you keep negative emotions under control before, during, and after meets?    1 2 3 4 5

*Character score:* _____

### *Humor*

13. Do you usually smile at your swimmers?    1 2 3 4 5

14. Are your practices fun?    1 2 3 4 5

15. Are you able to laugh at your mistakes?    1 2 3 4 5

*Humor score:* _____

If you scored 9 or less on any of the coaching tools, be sure to carefully reread the section describing it. And even if you scored 15 on every tool, don't be complacent. Keep learning! Then you'll be well-equipped with the tools you need to coach young athletes.

# How Should I Communicate With My Swimmers?

Now you know the tools you need to COACH: Comprehension, Outlook, Affection, Character, and Humor. These are essential for effective coaching, and without them you'd have a difficult time getting started. But none of these tools will work if you don't know how to use them with your athletes—that requires skillful communication. This unit examines what communication is and how you can become a more effective communicator-coach.

## What's Involved in Communication?

Coaches often think of communication as simply instructing athletes to do something, but verbal directions are a small part of the communication process. More than half of what is communicated in a message is non-verbal. So remember when you are coaching that actions do speak louder than words.

Communication in its simplest form involves two people: a *sender* and a *receiver*. The sender can transmit the message verbally, through facial expression, and by body language. Once the message is sent, the receiver tries to determine its meaning. A receiver who fails to attend or listen will miss part, if not all, of the message.

## How Can I Send More Effective Messages?

Young athletes often have little understanding of the rules and skills of swimming, and they probably have even less confidence in competing. So they need accurate, understandable, and supportive messages to help them along. That's why your verbal and nonverbal messages are so important.

### Verbal Messages

"Sticks and stones may break my bones, but words will never hurt me" isn't true. Spoken words can have a powerful and long-lasting effect. And coaches' words are particularly influential, because youngsters place great importance on what coaches say. Therefore,

whether you are correcting a misbehavior, teaching a swimmer how to execute a start, or praising a swimmer for good effort,

- *be positive, but honest;*
- *state it clearly and simply;*
- *say it loud enough and say it again; and*
- *be consistent.*

### Be Positive, But Honest

Nothing turns people off like hearing someone nag all the time. Young athletes are similarly discouraged by a coach who gripes constantly. The kids on your team need encouragement; many of them doubt their ability to race effectively. So *look* for and *tell* your swimmers what they did well.

On the other hand, don't cover up poor or incorrect actions with rosy words of praise. Kids know all too well when they've made a mistake, and no cheerfully expressed cliché can undo their errors. And if you fail to acknowledge swimmers' mistakes, your athletes will think you are a phony.

### State It Clearly and Simply

Positive and honest messages are good, but only if they're expressed directly and in words your athletes understand. Beating around the bush is ineffective and inefficient. If you

### Compliment Sandwich

A good way to handle situations where you have identified and must correct improper technique is to serve your swimmers a "compliment sandwich."

1. Point out what the swimmer did correctly.
2. Let the swimmer know what was incorrect in the performance and instruct her or him how to correct it.
3. Encourage the swimmer by reemphasizing what he or she did well.

ramble, your swimmers will miss the point of your message and lose interest. Here are some tips for saying things clearly:

- Organize your thoughts before you speak.
- Explain things thoroughly, but don't bore listeners with long-winded monologues.
- Use language that your swimmers can understand, but avoid trying to be "hip" by using their age group's slang.

### Say It Loud Enough and Say It Again

A swimming pool with children spread out from end to end can make communication difficult. So talk to your team in a voice that everyone can hear and interpret. It's okay, in fact appropriate, to soften your voice when speaking to a youngster individually about a personal problem. But most of the time your messages will be for all your swimmers to hear, so make sure they can! A word of caution, however: Don't dominate the setting with a booming voice that detracts attention from athletes' performances.

Sometimes what you say, even if stated loud and clear, won't sink in the first time. This may be particularly true with young athletes hearing words they don't understand. To avoid boring repetition but still get your message across, say the same thing in a slightly different way. For instance, you might first tell your swimmers, "Keep going until there is a recall rope on a false start."

Then, soon thereafter, remind them, "Don't stop if you *think* you heard a second beep." The second message may get through to some swimmers who missed it the first time around.

If you still aren't certain whether your swimmers understand, ask them to repeat the message back to you. As the saying goes, "If they can't say it, they can't do it."

### Be Consistent

People often say something in a way that implies a different message. For example, a touch of sarcasm added to the words "way to go" sends an entirely different message than the words themselves suggest. It is essential that you avoid sending such mixed messages. Keep the tone of your voice consistent with the words you use. And don't say something one day and contradict it the next; your swimmers will get confused.

## Nonverbal Messages

Just as you should be consistent in the tone of voice and words you use, you should also keep your verbal and nonverbal messages consistent. An example of failing to do this would be shaking your head, indicating disapproval, while at the same time telling a swimmer "nice try." Which is the youngster to believe, your gesture or your words?

Messages can be sent nonverbally in a number of ways. Facial expressions and body language are just two of the more obvious forms of nonverbal signals that can help you when you coach.

### Facial Expressions

The look on a person's face is the quickest clue to what he or she thinks or feels. Your swimmers know this, so they will study your face, looking for any sign that will tell them more than your words alone. Don't try to fool them by putting on a happy or blank "mask." They'll see through it, and you'll lose credibility.

Serious, stone-faced expressions are also of no help to kids who need cues about how they are performing. They will just assume you're unhappy or disinterested.

So don't be afraid to smile. A smile from a coach can boost the confidence of an unsure young athlete. Plus, a smile lets your players know that you are happy coaching them. But don't overdo it or your swimmers won't be able to tell when you are genuinely pleased by something they've done or when you are just "putting on" a smiling face.

### Body Language

How would your swimmers think you felt if you came to practice slouched over, with head down and shoulders slumped? Tired? Bored? Unhappy? How would they think you felt if you watched them during a meet with your hands on your hips, jaws clenched, and face reddened? Upset with them? Disgusted at an official? Mad at a parent?

Probably some or all of these things would enter your swimmers' minds. That's why you should carry yourself in a pleasant, confident, and vigorous manner. Such a posture not only projects happiness with your coaching role, it also provides a good example for your young athletes, who may imitate your behavior.

Physical contact can also be an important use of body language. A handshake, a pat on the head, an arm around the shoulder, even a big hug are effective ways of showing approval, concern, affection, and joy to your swimmers. Youngsters are especially in need of this type of nonverbal message. Keep within the obvious moral and legal limits, but don't be reluctant to touch your swimmers and send a message that can only truly be expressed in that way.

## How Can I Improve My Receiving Skills?

Now let's examine the other half of the communication process—receiving messages. Too often people are good senders but poor receivers of messages; they seem to enjoy hearing themselves talk more than listening to others. It is essential that as a coach of young athletes you receive their verbal and nonverbal messages effectively.

You can be a better receiver of your swimmers' messages if you are willing to read about the keys to receiving messages and then make a strong effort to use them with your athletes. You'll be surprised what you've been missing.

### Attention!

First, you must pay attention; you must want to hear what others have to communicate to you. That's not always easy when you're busy coaching and many things are competing for your attention. But in one-to-one or team meetings with youngsters, you must really focus on what they are telling you, both verbally and nonverbally. Not only will such focused attention help you catch every word they say, but you'll also notice their moods and physical states, and you'll get an idea of their feelings toward you and other members of the team.

### Listen CARE-FULLY

How we receive a message, perhaps more than anything else we do, demonstrates how much we care for the sender and what that person has to tell us. If you care little for your swimmers or have little regard for what they have to say, it will show in how you attend and listen to them.

Check yourself. Do you find your mind wandering to what you are going to do after practice while an athlete is talking to you? Do you frequently have to ask your swimmers "What did you say?" If so, you need to work on your receiving mechanics of attending and listening. If you find that you're missing the messages your swimmers send, perhaps the most critical question you should ask yourself is this: Do I care?

## How Do I Put It All Together?

So far we've discussed separately the sending and receiving of messages. But we all know that senders and receivers switch roles several times during an interaction. One person initiates a communication by sending a message to another person, who then receives the message. The receiver then switches roles and becomes the sender by responding to the person who sent the initial message. These verbal and nonverbal responses are called feedback.

Your swimmers will be looking to you for feedback all the time. They will want to know how you think they are performing, what you think of their ideas, and whether their efforts

please you. How you respond will strongly affect your swimmers. So let's take a look at a few general types of feedback and examine their possible effects.

### Providing Instructions

With young swimmers, much of your feedback will involve answering questions about how to swim better. Your instructive responses should include both verbal and nonverbal feedback. The following are suggestions for giving instructional feedback:

- Keep verbal instructions simple and concise.
- Use demonstrations to provide nonverbal instructional feedback (see Unit 4).
- Walk swimmers through the skill step by step, or use a slow-motion demonstration if they are having trouble learning.

### Correcting Errors

When your athletes perform incorrectly, you need to provide informative feedback to remedy the error—and the sooner the better. And when you do correct errors, keep in mind these two principles: Use negative criticism sparingly, and stay calm.

#### Use Negative Criticism Sparingly

Although you may need to punish youngsters for horseplay or dangerous activities by scolding or temporarily removing them from activity, avoid reprimanding swimmers for performance errors. Admonishing swimmers for honest mistakes makes them afraid to even try; nothing ruins a youngster's enjoyment of a sport more than a coach who harps on every miscue. So instead, correct your athletes by using the positive approach. They'll enjoy swimming more, and you'll enjoy coaching more.

#### Keep Calm

Don't fly off the handle when your swimmers make mistakes. Remember, you're coaching young and inexperienced athletes, not pros, so you'll see more incorrect than correct

a youngster's confidence. And a pat on the back or a handshake can be a very tangible way of communicating your recognition of a swimmer's performance.

### Coaches, be positive!

Only a very small percentage of ASEP-trained coaches' behaviors are negative.

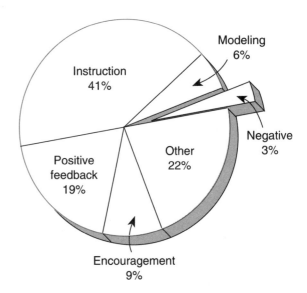

technique and probably have more discipline problems than you expect. But throwing a tantrum over each error or misbehavior will only inhibit your swimmers and model for them the wrong kind of behavior to follow. Let your team know that mistakes aren't the end of the world; stay cool!

### Positive Feedback

Praising swimmers when they have performed or behaved well is an effective way of getting them to repeat (or try to repeat) that behavior in the future. And positive feedback for effort is an especially effective way to motivate youngsters to work on difficult skills. So rather than shouting and providing negative feedback to a swimmer who has made a mistake, try offering a compliment sandwich (described on page 12).

Sometimes just the way you word feedback can make it more positive than negative. For example, instead of saying "Don't push off the wall like that," you might say, "Streamline your pushoff." Then your swimmers will be focusing on *what to do* instead of what *not* to do.

You can give positive feedback verbally and nonverbally. Telling a swimmer, especially in front of teammates, that she or he has performed well is a great way to increase

## Who Else Do I Need to Communicate With?

Coaching not only involves sending and receiving messages and providing proper feedback to swimmers, it also includes interacting with swimmers' parents, officials, and opposing coaches. So try these suggestions for communicating with each group.

### Parents

A swimmer's parents need to be assured that their son or daughter is under the direction of a coach who is both knowledgeable about swimming and concerned about the youngster's well-being. You can put their worries to rest by holding a preseason parent orientation meeting in which you describe your background and your approach to coaching.

If a parent contacts you with a concern during the season, listen closely and try to offer a positive response. If you need to

communicate with parents, catch them after a practice, call, or send a note through the mail. Messages sent through children are too often lost, misinterpreted, or forgotten.

## Officials

How you communicate with officials greatly influences the way your swimmers behave toward them, so you need to set a positive example. Greet officials with a handshake, an introduction, and perhaps some casual conversation about the upcoming meet. Indicate your respect for them before, during, and after the meet.

Keep in mind that most youth swimming officials are volunteers or are working for a nominal fee. So don't make nasty remarks, shout, or use disrespectful body gestures. Your swimmers will see you do it, and they'll get the idea that such behavior is appropriate. Plus, if the official hears or sees you, the communication between you will break down. In short, you take care of the coaching, and let the officials run the swim meet.

## Opposing Coaches

Make an effort to visit with the coach of the opposing team before the meet. Perhaps the two of you can work out a special arrangement for the meet, such as allowing exhibition swimmers to compete in some events. Don't get into a personal feud with the opposing coach during the meet. Remember, it's the kids, not the coaches, who are competing.

## Summary Checklist

Check your communication skills by answering yes or no to the following questions.

|  | Yes | No |
|---|---|---|
| 1. Are your verbal messages to your swimmers positive and honest? | ___ | ___ |
| 2. Do you speak loudly, clearly, and in a language your athletes understand? | ___ | ___ |
| 3. Do you remember to repeat instructions to your swimmers, in case they didn't hear or understand you the first time? | ___ | ___ |
| 4. Are your tone of voice and your nonverbal messages consistent with the words you use? | ___ | ___ |
| 5. Do your facial expressions and body language express interest in and happiness with your coaching role? | ___ | ___ |
| 6. Are you attentive to swimmers and able to pick up even their small verbal and nonverbal cues? | ___ | ___ |
| 7. Do you really care about what your athletes say to you? | ___ | ___ |
| 8. Do you instruct rather than criticize when your swimmers make errors? | ___ | ___ |

9. Are you usually positive when responding to things your athletes say and do?     ___ ___

10. Do you try to communicate in a cooperative and respectful manner with parents, officials, and opposing coaches?     ___ ___

If you answered no to any of these questions, you may want to refer back to the section of the chapter where the topic was discussed. *Now* is the time to address communication problems, not when you're coaching your swimmers.

UNIT
4

# How Do I Get My Team Ready to Compete?

To coach swimming, you must understand the basic rules, skills, and techniques of the sport. The second part of this *Rookie Coaches Swimming Guide* provides the basic information you'll need to comprehend swimming.

But all the swimming knowledge in the world will do you little good unless you present it effectively to your athletes. That's why this unit is so important. In it you will learn the steps to take in teaching sport skills as well as practical guidelines for planning your season and individual practices.

## How Do I Teach Swimming Skills?

Many people believe that the only qualification needed to coach is to have competed in a sport. It's helpful to have been a swimmer, but there is much more to coaching successfully.

And even if you haven't swum competitively, you can still teach the skills of the sport effectively using this IDEA:

I — Introduce the skill.

D — Demonstrate the skill.

E — Explain the skill.

A — Attend to swimmers practicing the skill.

## Introduce the Skill

Swimmers, especially young and inexperienced ones, need to know what skill they are learning and why. To make things clear, you should take these three steps every time you introduce a skill to your swimmers:

1. Get all swimmers' attention.
2. Name the skill.
3. Explain the skill's importance.

### Get All Swimmers' Attention

Because youngsters are easily distracted, use some effective method to get their attention. Some coaches use interesting news items or stories. Others use jokes. Still others simply project an enthusiasm that invites athletes to listen. Whatever method you use, speak slightly above the normal volume and make eye contact with swimmers when you speak.

It helps if you arrange the swimmers in two or three evenly spaced rows, facing you and not some source of distraction (a classroom setting is ideal). At the least, use a neutral setting like a blank wall to stand in front of, with all the athletes facing you. Then check that everyone can see and hear you before you begin.

### Name the Skill

Although you might mention other common names for the skill, decide which one you'll use and stick with it. This will help avoid confusion and enhance communication with your swimmers. For example, choose either "freestyle" or "crawl" as the term for that stroke, and use it consistently.

### Explain the Importance of the Skill

Although the importance of a skill may be apparent to you, your athletes may be less able to see how the skill will help them become better swimmers. Offer a reason for learning the skill and describe how it relates to more advanced skills. For instance, explain that the freestyle is the most effective stroke for training. Then explain that the freestyle is also used at the end of the individual medley (IM) events and has four times as many events as any other stroke.

---

*The most difficult aspect of coaching is this: Coaches must learn to let athletes learn. Sport skills should be taught so they have meaning to the child, not just meaning to the coach.*

Rainer Martens, ASEP Founder

---

## Demonstrate the Skill

Demonstration is the most important part of teaching a swimming skill to young athletes who may have never done anything like it. They need a picture, not just words. They need to *see* how the skill is performed. And presenting the picture right the first time is worth a great deal. Much physical skill learning is visual.

If you cannot perform the skill correctly yourself, have an assistant coach or someone skilled in swimming give the demonstration. A high school varsity swimmer would be an excellent choice. Age-group swimmers also make great demonstrators. These teenage swimmers can be especially effective with younger athletes because the older kids are the local "pool heroes" and role models. These tips will help make your demonstrations more effective:

- Use correct form.
- Demonstrate the skill several times.
- Slow down the skill, if possible, during one or two performances so swimmers can see every movement involved.
- Perform the skill at different angles so your swimmers can get a full perspective of it.

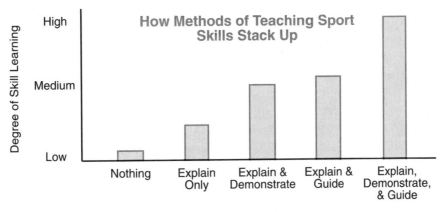

**How Methods of Teaching Sport Skills Stack Up**

Y-axis: Degree of Skill Learning (Low, Medium, High)

X-axis (Coach Teaching Method): Nothing; Explain Only; Explain & Demonstrate; Explain & Guide; Explain, Demonstrate, & Guide

If you don't have access to an accomplished swimmer to demonstrate the skills, a videotape (there are many good ones on the market) can substitute well.

## Explain the Skill

Swimmers learn a skill more effectively when they're given a brief explanation along with the demonstration. Use simple terms to describe the skill, and if possible relate it to previously learned skills. Verbal presentations are usually hard for novice swimmers to follow. Try to talk a little and show a lot. Ask your swimmers if they understand your description. If someone looks confused, have him or her explain the skill back to you.

Complex skills often are better understood if they are explained in more manageable parts. For instance, if you want to teach your swimmers how to swim butterfly, you might take the following steps:

1. Show them a correct performance of the entire skill and explain that butterfly is the first stroke in the IM.
2. Break down the stroke and point out its component parts.
3. Have swimmers perform each of the component skills you have already taught them, such as leg action and kick, body position, arm action and recovery, and rhythm and breathing.
4. After swimmers have demonstrated their ability to perform the components in sequence, reexplain the entire skill.
5. Have swimmers practice the skill.

## Attend to Swimmers Practicing the Skill

If the skill you selected was within your athletes' capabilities and you have done an effective job of introducing, demonstrating, and explaining, your swimmers should be ready to try it. Some swimmers may need to be physically guided through the movements during their first few attempts. It will take time to develop proficiency.

For example, some swimmers may need your hands-on help to learn where to breathe in the stroke cycle. Guiding unsure athletes through the skill in this way will help them gain confidence to perform it on their own.

Your teaching duties don't end when all your athletes have demonstrated that they understand how to perform the skill. In fact, a significant part of your teaching will involve

observing closely the hit-and-miss trial performances of your swimmers.

As you observe swimmers' efforts in drills and activities, offer positive, corrective feedback in the form of the compliment sandwich described in Unit 3. If a swimmer performs the skill properly, acknowledge it and offer praise. Keep in mind that your feedback will have a great influence on youngsters' motivation to practice and improve their skills.

Remember, too, that young swimmers need individual instruction. So set aside a time before, during, or after practice to give individual help.

## What Planning Do I Need to Do?

Beginning coaches often make the mistake of showing up for the first practice with no particular plan in mind. These coaches find that their practices are unorganized, their swimmers are frustrated and inattentive, and the amount and quality of their skill instruction is limited. Planning is essential to successful teaching *and* coaching. And it doesn't begin on the way to practice!

### Preseason Planning

Effective coaches begin planning well before the start of the season. Among the preseason measures that will make the season more enjoyable, successful, and safe for you and your swimmers are the following:

- Familiarize yourself with the sport organization you are involved in, especially its philosophy and goals regarding youth sport.
- Examine the availability of facilities, equipment, instructional aids, and other materials needed for practices and meets.
- Check to see if you have liability insurance to cover you should a swimmer get hurt (see Unit 5). If you don't, get some.
- Establish your coaching priorities regarding having fun, developing swimmers' skills, and winning.
- Select and meet with your assistant coaches to discuss the philosophy, goals, team rules, and plans for the season.

- Register swimmers for the team. Have them complete a swimmer information form and obtain medical clearance forms, if required.
- Institute an injury-prevention program for your swimmers.
- Hold a parent orientation meeting to describe your background, philosophy, goals, and instructional approach. Also, give a brief overview of the league's rules, terms, and meet procedures to familiarize parents or guardians with the sport.

You may be surprised at the number of things you should do even before the first practice. But addressing these points during the preseason will make the season much more enjoyable and productive for you and your swimmers.

### In-Season Planning

Your choice of activities during the season should be based on whether they will help your athletes develop physical and mental skills, knowledge of rules and techniques, sportsmanship, and love for swimming. All of these goals are important, but we'll focus on the skills and techniques of swimming to give you an idea of how to itemize your objectives.

### Goal Setting

What you plan to do during the season must be reasonable for the maturity and skill level of your swimmers. In terms of skills and techniques, you should teach young swimmers the basics and move on to more complex activities only after they have mastered these easier techniques.

To begin the season, you might set the following instructional goals:

- Swimmers will be able to get into the ready position on the blocks.
- Swimmers will be able to assume an effective stance when starting.
- Swimmers will be able to legally swim four strokes.
- Swimmers will be able to compete in a 100 IM.
- Swimmers will be able to use proper mechanics when starting and turning.
- Swimmers will be able to communicate with teammates.
- Swimmers will develop a respect for teamwork.
- Swimmers will swim hard and have fun at the same time.
- Swimmers will develop confidence in their abilities.
- Swimmers will show respect for officials, coaches, and other swimmers.
- Swimmers will learn how to win with class and how to be good losers.
- Swimmers will show good sportsmanship at all times.
- Swimmers will be able to practice and compete safely.
- Swimmers will demonstrate knowledge of swimming rules.

### Organizing

After you've defined the skills and techniques you want swimmers to learn during the season, you can plan how to teach them in practices. But be flexible! If your swimmers are having difficulty learning a skill or technique, take some extra time until they get the hang of it—even if that means moving back your schedule. After all, if your swimmers are unable to perform the fundamental skills, they'll never execute the more complex skills you have scheduled.

Still, it helps to have a plan for progressing athletes through skills during the season. The 8-week sample lesson plan in the Appendix shows how to schedule your skill instruction in an organized and progressive manner. If this is your first coaching experience, you may wish to follow the plan as it stands. If you have some previous experience, you may want to modify the schedule to better fit the needs of your team.

## What Makes Up a Good Practice?

A good instructional plan makes practice preparation much easier. Have swimmers work on more important and less difficult goals in early season practice sessions. And see to it that swimmers master basic skills before moving on to more advanced ones.

It is helpful to establish one objective for each practice, but try to include a variety of activities related to that objective. This can make an otherwise boring swimming practice fun. For example, although your primary objective might be to improve the freestyle turn, you should have swimmers perform several different drills designed to enhance that single skill. And, to inject further variety into your practices, vary the order of the activities you schedule for swimmers to perform.

In general, we recommend that each of your practices include the following steps:

- *Warm up*
- *Practice previously taught skills*
- *Teach and practice new skills*
- *Cool down*
- *Evaluate*

### Warm Up

As you're checking the roster and announcing the performance objectives for the practice, your swimmers should be preparing their bodies for vigorous activity. A 5- to 10-minute period of easy-paced swims, kicks and pulling drills, stretching, and calisthenics should be sufficient for youngsters to limber their muscles and reduce the risk of injury.

### Practice Previously Taught Skills

Devote part of each practice to having swimmers work on the fundamental skills they already know. But remember, children like variety. So organize and modify drills to keep everyone involved and interested. Praise and encourage swimmers when you notice improvement, and offer individual assistance to those who need help.

### Teach and Practice New Skills

Gradually build on your swimmers' existing skills by giving them something new to practice each session. The proper method for teaching swimming skills is described on pages 19 to 22. Refer to those pages if you have any questions about teaching new skills or if you want to evaluate your teaching approach periodically during the season.

### Cool Down

Each practice should wind down with a 5- to 10-minute period of easy continuous swimming. The cool-down allows athletes' bodies to return to the resting state and avoid stiffness, and it gives you an opportunity to review the practice.

### Evaluate

At the end of practice spend a few minutes with your swimmers reviewing how well the session accomplished the objective you had set. Even if your evaluation is negative, show optimism for future practices and send players off on an upbeat note.

## How Do I Put a Practice Together?

Simply knowing the five practice components is not enough. You must also be able to arrange those components into a logical progression and fit them into a time schedule. Using your instructional goals as a guide for selecting what skills to have your swimmers work on, try to plan several swim practices you might conduct. The following example should help you get started.

## *Sample Practice Plan*

*Performance Objective.* Swimmers will be able to recover the hand close to the body and close to the water.

| Component | Time | Activity or drill |
|---|---|---|
| Warm up | 5 min | Easy swimming<br>Stretching |
| Teach | 10 min | Freestyle recovery drills<br>Hand-entry drill |
| Practice previously learned skills | 10 min | Freestyle pull drills<br>Streamlining pushoffs |
| Do conditioning drills | 10 min | Turning drills, freestyle, and backstroke |
|  | 15 min | $3 \times 100$ on 15 seconds' rest<br>$10 \times 50$ on 10 seconds' rest |
| Cool down and evaluate | 5 min | Easy swimming<br>Stretching |
| Do quick review | 5 min |  |
| Give reminder about next practice | 5 min |  |

## Summary Checklist

During the swimming season, check your teaching and planning skills periodically. As you gain more coaching experience, you should be able to answer yes to each of the following questions:

*When you plan, do you remember to plan for*

____ preseason events like swimmer registration, liability protection, use of facilities, and parent orientation?

____ season goals, such as developing swimmers' physical and mental skills, fostering sportsmanship, and having fun?

____ practice components such as warm-up, practicing previously taught skills, teaching and practicing new skills, cool-down, and evaluation?

*When you teach skills to your swimmers, do you*

____ arrange the athletes so all can see and hear?

____ introduce the skill clearly and explain its importance?

____ demonstrate the skill properly several times?

____ explain the skill simply and accurately?

____ attend closely to swimmers practicing the skill?

____ offer corrective, positive feedback or praise after observing swimmers' attempts at the skill?

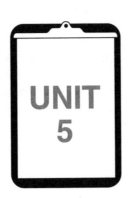

# UNIT 5

# *What Can I Do for Safety?*

One of your new swimmers has never started from a platform before, and the pool you are to compete in next week is equipped with them. What will you do this week to get your swimmer ready to complete her starting dive safely?

One of the most unpleasant aspects of coaching is seeing athletes get hurt. Fortunately, there are many preventive measures you can institute to reduce the risk. But in spite of such efforts, injury remains a reality of sport participation, and you must be prepared to provide first aid when injuries occur and to protect yourself against unjustified lawsuits. This unit will describe how you can

- create the safest possible environment for your swimmers,

- provide emergency first aid to swimmers when they get hurt, and
- protect yourself from injury liability.

## How Do I Keep My Swimmers From Getting Hurt?

Injuries may occur because of poor preventive measures. Part of your planning, described in Unit 4, should include steps that give your swimmers the best possible chance for injury-free participation. These steps include the following:

- *Preseason physical examination*
- *Physical conditioning*
- *Equipment and facilities inspection*
- *Matching swimmers by physical ability and warning of inherent risks*
- *Liability waivers*
- *Proper supervision and record keeping*
- *Sufficient hydration*
- *Warm-up and cool-down*

### Preseason Physical Examination

Even in the absence of severe injury or ongoing illness, your swimmers should have physical examinations every 2 years. Any swimmer with a known complication should obtain a physician's consent before participation is allowed. You should also have each swimmer's parents or guardians sign a participation agreement form and a release form to allow their daughter or son to be treated in the case of an emergency.

### Physical Conditioning

Muscles, tendons, and ligaments unaccustomed to vigorous and long-lasting physical activity are prone to injury, so it is important to prepare your athletes to withstand the exertion of competitive swimming. An effective conditioning program would include both aerobic and anaerobic conditioning.

Make conditioning drills and activities fun. Include a skill component, such as stroke drills, to prevent swimmers from becoming bored or looking upon the activity as "work."

### Equipment and Facilities Inspection

Another means to prevent injuries is to inspect for wear and other safety hazards all the tools your swimmers will be using—kickboards, fins, resistance tubing, and so on. And remember to instruct your team in the appropriate use of equipment. For example, resistance tubing should be used only under your supervision.

Remember to examine, before and after each workout, the pool where your swimmers practice and compete. Remove hazards, report conditions you cannot remedy, and request maintenance as necessary. The pool must always be clear when you begin practice and clear when you leave. Be sure to review with your team all the safety aspects associated with the pool where you work out. Remember, your first obligation is safety.

### Matching Swimmers by Ability and Warning of Inherent Risks

Children of the same age may differ in height and weight by up to 6 inches and 50 pounds. These differences present no inherent danger in swimming because the sport is noncontact, but it is important that you

group athletes with others of similar ability. This prevents the faster swimmers from "swimming over" the slower ones during the course of a workout.

Matching helps protect you from certain liability concerns. But you also must warn swimmers of the inherent risks involved in swimming, because "failure to warn" is one of the most successful arguments in lawsuits against coaches. So thoroughly explain the inherent risks of swimming and make sure each swimmer knows, understands, and appreciates those risks.

## Liability Waivers

The preseason parent orientation meeting is a good opportunity to explain the risks of the sport to parents and swimmers. It is also a good time to have both swimmers and parents sign waivers releasing you from liability should an injury occur. Such waivers do not discharge you from responsibility for your swimmers' well-being, but they are recommended by attorneys.

## Proper Supervision and Record Keeping

With youngsters, your mere presence in the pool area is not enough; you must actively plan and direct team activities and closely observe and evaluate swimmers' participation. You're the watchdog responsible for their welfare. So if you notice a swimmer grimacing or struggling, give her or him a rest and check to see if there is an injury or if the youngster simply needed a break.

As a coach, you're also required to enforce the rules of the sport, prohibit dangerous horseplay, and hold practices only under safe weather conditions. These specific supervisory activities will make the environment safer for your swimmers and help protect you from liability should an injury occur.

For further protection, keep records of your season plans, practice plans, and swimmers' injuries. Season and practice plans come in handy when you need evidence that swimmers have been taught certain skills;

---

### Informed Consent Form

I hereby give my permission for _____ to participate in

_____ during the athletic season beginning in 199___. Further, I authorize the school to provide emergency treatment of an injury to or illness of my child if qualified medical personnel consider treatment necessary *and* perform the treatment. This authorization is granted only if I cannot be reached and a reasonable effort has been made to do so.

Date _____  Parent or guardian _____

Address _____  Phone ( ) _____

Family physician _____  Phone ( ) _____

Pre-existing medical conditions (e.g., allergies or chronic illnesses) _____

_____

Other(s) to also contact in case of emergency _____

Relationship to child _____  Phone ( ) _____

My child and I are aware that participating in _____ is a potentially hazardous activity. I assume all risks associated with participation in this sport, including but not limited to falls, contact with other participants, the effects of the weather, traffic, and other reasonable risk conditions associated with the sport. All such risks to my child are known and understood by me.

I understand this informed consent form and agree to its conditions on behalf of my child.

Child's signature _____  Date_____

Parent's signature _____  Date_____

accurate, detailed accident reports offer protection against unfounded lawsuits. Ask for these forms from the organization to which you belong. Hold on to these records for several years so an "old swimming injury" of a former athlete doesn't come back to haunt you.

## Sufficient Hydration

You may not be aware that an athlete working hard in the water does sweat and build up heat. Swimmers need a ready supply of cool water to keep from dehydrating. And they may need a reminder from you to take breaks and drink some water, because by the time they are aware of their thirst, they are long overdue for a drink. Young swimmers are particularly unaware of their own need for fluid, so enforce water consumption from individual squeeze bottles kept right by the side of the pool.

## Warm-Up and Cool-Down

Although young bodies are generally very limber, they also can get tight from inactivity. A warm-up period of about 10 minutes before each practice is strongly recommended. Warm-up should address each muscle group and get the heart rate elevated in preparation for strenuous activity. A common sequence is easy swimming or drills followed by these stretching exercises (hold each stretch for 20 seconds, then release):

**Side and Shoulder Stretches**—Stand with one arm extended straight up, then tilt the upper body to the opposite side, reaching the hand up and across the head. Repeat the stretch on the other side. For the shoulder stretch, extend one arm across the chest, grasp the raised elbow with the opposite hand, and pull the elbow in the direction of the hand (see Figure 5.1). Repeat the stretch on the other side.

**Triceps Stretch**—Sit or stand upright with one arm bent and raised overhead next to the ear, hand resting on the shoulder blade. Grasp the elbow with the opposite hand and pull it behind your head. Switch arms and repeat the stretch.

**Shoulder Circle Stretch**—Stand upright and make *slow* circles with one arm, with the

**Figure 5.1**   The shoulder stretch.

hand passing directly over the shoulder. Keep the arm straight. Slowly increase in speed, using the fist as an "end weight." Do four forward and four backward circles. Repeat with the other arm.

**Partner Shoulder Stretch**—A partner clasps the athlete's hands palm to palm, with thumbs up, and slowly pulls the arms back directly behind the shoulders. Hold at a maximum stretch for 5 seconds, then repeat three to five times.

**Lower Back Stretch**—Stand upright and then reach over to touch the toes, being careful not to bounce. Repeat 6 to 10 times, trying to reach farther each time. This stretch may be done with a partner assisting.

**Hip Flexor Stretch**—Assume a kneeling lunge position, with the left leg and top of the foot against the floor and the right knee bent and the sole of the right foot on the floor. With hands on hips, lean forward, pressing the left hip toward the floor; keep chest and shoulders upright (see Figure 5.2). Repeat the stretch on the other side.

**Figure 5.2**   The hip flexor stretch.

**Hamstring Stretch**—Sit upright on the floor. Bend the right knee and slide the heel toward the buttocks until it is against the inner side of the left thigh (a 90-degree angle should be formed between the extended left leg and bent right leg). Keeping the left leg straight, bend at the waist and lower the torso toward the straight leg (see Figure 5.3). Switch legs and repeat the stretch.

**Figure 5.3** The hamstring stretch.

As practice is winding down, slow swimmers' heart rates with an easy swim or kick. Then arrange for 5 or 10 minutes of easy stretching at the end of practice to help swimmers avoid stiff muscles and make them less tight before the next practice.

## What If One of My Swimmers Gets Hurt?

No matter how good and thorough your prevention program, injuries will occur. And when injury does strike, chances are you will be the one in charge. The severity and nature of the injury will determine how involved you'll be in treating it. But regardless of how seriously a swimmer is hurt, it is your responsibility to know what steps to take. You and your staff should know the emergency action plan that is in effect at the pool you use. If there is no such plan, the pool manager needs to develop one. In an emergency, knowing who will do what when will save a life.

Before beginning your swim coaching career, you should complete a course in CPR (cardiopulmonary resuscitation), first aid, and safety training for swim coaches. ASEP offers a comprehensive Sport First Aid course, which includes clinic, self-study, and testing phases. The American Red Cross and the YMCA offer safety training courses specifically for swim coaches. Contact these organizations for more information about the courses on this essential topic.

Within the scope of this book, we'll take a look at how you can provide *basic* emergency care to your injured athletes. This information should not be a substitute for taking the classes just mentioned.

### Minor Injuries

Although no injury seems unimportant to the person experiencing it, most injuries are neither life-threatening nor severe enough to restrict participation. And when such injuries occur, you can take an active role in their initial treatment.

### Scrapes and Cuts

When a swimmer has an open wound, the first thing you should do is to put on a pair of disposable surgical gloves or some other effective blood barrier. Then follow these three steps:

1. Stop the bleeding by applying direct pressure with a clean dressing to the wound and elevating it. *Do not* remove the dressing if it becomes blood-soaked. Instead, place an additional dressing on top of the one already in place. If bleeding continues, elevate the injured area above the heart and maintain pressure. Then have the swimmer receive trained medical attention.
2. Cleanse the wound thoroughly once the bleeding is controlled. A good rinsing with a forceful stream of water and perhaps light scrubbing with soap will help prevent infection.
3. Protect the wound with sterile gauze or a bandage strip.

For a bloody nose not associated with serious facial injury, have the athlete sit and lean slightly forward. Then pinch the athlete's nostrils shut. If the bleeding continues after several minutes or if the athlete has a history of nosebleeds, seek medical assistance.

## The PRICE Method

**P** — Protect the athlete and the injured body part from danger or further trauma.

**R** — Rest the area to avoid further damage and to foster healing.

**I** — Ice the area to reduce swelling and pain.

**C** — Compress the area by securing an ice bag in place with an elastic wrap.

**E** — Elevate the injury above heart level to keep the blood from pooling in the area.

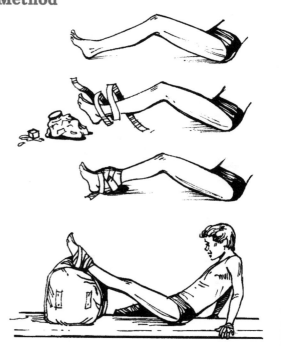

### Sprains and Strains

If a swimmer suffers a minor injury to a muscle or tendon (a strain) or to a ligament (a sprain), immediately apply the PRICE method of injury care.

### Serious Injuries

Head and spine injuries, fractures, and injuries that cause swimmers to lose consciousness are among a class of injuries that you cannot and should not try to treat yourself. But you should plan what you'll do if such an injury occurs. Your plan should include the following guidelines for action:

- In advance, get the phone numbers and ensure the availability of nearby emergency care units.
- Assign an assistant coach or another adult the responsibility of contacting emergency medical help upon your request.
- Do not move the injured athlete.
- Calm the injured athlete and keep others away from him or her as much as possible.

- Evaluate whether the athlete's breathing is stopped or irregular and, if necessary, clear the airway with your fingers.
- Administer artificial respiration if breathing has stopped.
- Administer CPR, or have a trained individual administer CPR, if the athlete's circulation has stopped.
- Remain with the athlete until medical personnel arrive.

## How Do I Protect Myself?

When one of your swimmers is injured, naturally your first concern is her or his well-being. Your feelings for children, after all, are what led you to coach. Unfortunately, there is something else that you must consider: Can you be held liable for the injury?

From a legal standpoint, a coach has nine duties to fulfill. We've discussed all but planning (see Unit 4) in this unit.

1. Provide a safe environment.

2. Properly plan the activity.

3. Provide adequate and proper equipment.

4. Match or equate athletes.

5. Warn of inherent risks in the sport.

6. Supervise the activity closely.

7. Evaluate athletes for injury or incapacity.

8. Know emergency procedures and first aid.

9. Keep adequate records.

In addition to fulfilling these nine legal duties, you should check your insurance coverage to make sure your present policy will protect you from liability.

## Summary Self-Test

Now that you've read how to make your coaching experience safe for your swimmers and yourself, test your knowledge of the material by answering these questions:

1. What eight injury prevention measures can you institute?
2. What is the three-step emergency care process for cuts?
3. What method of treatment is best for minor sprains and strains?
4. What steps can you take to manage serious injuries?
5. What are the nine legal duties of a coach?

# UNIT 6

# *What Is Swimming All About?*

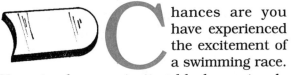

**C**hances are you have experienced the excitement of a swimming race. You stand on a starting block, anxiously awaiting the horn that will send you hurtling into the water. As your legs begin the drive to leap, your arms stretch forward to aim for the entry spot. You dive in and come up swimming hard, maintaining a steady cadence. You bring it home strong, and at the finish you're breathing hard and your arms feel like rubber. But you're filled with the exhilaration of moving through water with speed.

Now it's time for you to share your love of swimming with your team. From reading the first part of this book, you have a good overview of what it takes to be a coach. The next three units of the *Rookie Coaches Swimming Guide* will provide you the swimming-specific information you need to work with developing swimmers. Included are the basic skills, techniques, and drills that you should teach your young charges.

In this unit we'll explore the various components of competitive swimming. As a coach, you'll be concerned with the conduct of your athletes in both team practices and competitive meets. The pleasure and success of your team will depend on your skill in both settings.

## The Rules

Most swim meets are conducted under the rules of United States Swimming, the national governing body for the sport. Some are conducted under YMCA rules, which closely mimic the rules of the National College Athletic Association and National Federation of State High School Associations. The actual swimming rules are beyond the scope of this text, so as early in the year as possible you should obtain a set of the rules that govern your league and become knowledgeable about them. Generally, each set of rules has one section that governs how the strokes are executed and another that determines the conduct of meets. Don't assume because you swam yourself that you are familiar with all the rules, because they undergo continual change. You need to familiarize yourself with both sections, and your athletes need to learn the rules for swimming the strokes legally.

## Swimming Pools

Swim meets are conducted in two types of facilities, commonly known as long course (50-meter) and short course (25-yard) pools. Occasionally you will come across a 25-meter pool, which is also called short course. Olympic swimming events are held in a 50-meter long course pool. Most summer league swimmers compete in short course facilities.

## Swimming Equipment

A variety of swimming gear is available that you may decide to have your team use to improve their performance in the pool. Here are descriptions of some of the most common pieces of gear:

**Goggles** reduce eye irritation from water chemistry and provide better underwater vision.

A **kickboard** is an aid that lets swimmers work only the legs to strengthen those muscles (see Figure 6.1a); essential tool for stroke drills.

**Pace clocks and stopwatches** are used to time events, segments of practice, and so on.

A **pullbuoy** goes between the legs to immobilize and float them, allowing the swimmer to use arms only (see Figure 6.1b).

A **swimming vest** goes on like a lifejacket to provide additional water resistance to improve strength.

A **stretch cord** ties on one end to a belt around the swimmer's waist and on the other around a solid part of the pool or starting block; the swimmer swims hard, and the cord provides increasing resistance.

Hand-held **swim paddles** attach with loops of tubing to the swimmer's hands, increasing the surface area that is pulled against and building strength and feel for the water (see Figure 6.1c).

**Video cameras and housings** provide a crucial learning and teaching tool; underwater and "periscope" housings are available for the invaluable underwater view. Commercially produced videos of Olympic and international-calibre swimmers are an inexpensive way for the rookie coach to show and educate swimmers about good technique. Most of these tapes come with expert narration.

Many other types of gear can be found in swimming magazines and in catalogs from swim suppliers. All the gear has some useful purpose, and you should consider the items as coaching tools.

## Practices

In contrast to other sports your young athletes may have done, swimming emphasizes practices over competitive opportunities. One reason for this approach is that it takes time to develop the skills necessary to make competition a worthwhile experience. It's no fun

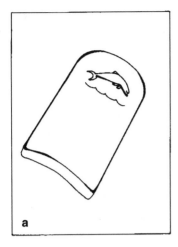  

**Figure 6.1** Common swimming gear: (a) kickboard, (b) pullbuoy, and (c) swim paddles.

competing in a swim meet until you can do it with some degree of capability by having spent time in planned, progressive activities.

You will coach best in practice

   . . . by having a plan for teaching and learning skills.

   . . . by giving each child a chance to develop at her own pace.

   . . . by offering primarily positive, self-image-enhancing feedback.

   . . . by allowing each child a chance to show what he does best.

   . . . by finding ways to showcase each child's skills—some in the water, some out.

   . . . by allowing each child a time to lead and a time to follow. (You can accomplish this easily by changing lane assignments daily.)

When you conduct practice, everyone in the pool must understand that you are in charge. Because water always holds the potential for danger, it must be clear that while you want to have fun in practice, your leadership is absolute. Your swimmers must always follow your instructions without question. The time for questions is when everyone is safe and dry on the deck. If you have assistants, make sure they understand and enforce this policy, too.

### What to Cover in Practices

With a novice summer-league swim team, close to 90% of your practice time should be spent teaching. And as you are teaching and drilling your swimmers, they will improve in conditioning.

At a minimum, you'll want to teach the following skills:

- **Strokes:** freestyle, backstroke, breaststroke, butterfly
- **Starts:** forward start, backstroke start, relay start
- **Turns:** freestyle "flip" turn, backstroke turn, breaststroke turn, butterfly turn, IM turns (fly/back, back/breast, breast/free)

Covering every skill in this list is plenty for a summer or a 2-month season. Much of what you'll teach will be dictated by the initial levels of your swimmers. Most novice teams will have swimmers with a range of abilities, from pretty good but unsophisticated in skills to barely out of a learn-to-swim program. You'll need to tailor your teaching to every swimmer. It's a great challenge and one of the most enjoyable parts of your coaching job!

### Swim Meets

Swim meets, an important part of the swimming experience, are one place where your coaching will be under scrutiny from the people who employ you. A thorough understanding of how best to serve your swimmers will be much appreciated by your team and your employers.

## Who Conducts Swim Meets?

In the United States, a variety of hosts conduct swim meets. Most coaches start their work in summer league teams, where the meets are run by a committee of parents or a recreation supervisor. These meets are relatively simple to operate and fun for everyone.

The YMCA also conducts age group swimming competitions, and the rules and regulations as well as the officiating in these events are marked by much greater sophistication. If you are a USS or YMCA coach, a full study of the organization's rulebook is a must.

Most new coaches will work under relatively loose rules modeled on USS or YMCA formats, with some relaxed interpretation in summer swimming. Your knowledge of the specific rules is vital to your success, but a full explanation is beyond the scope of this text. You should immediately obtain a copy of the relevant rules upon notification of your job assignment.

## The Purposes of Swim Meets

The first purpose for swim meets is *competition*, whose meaning derives from the Greek— to "strive with." This striving produces improvements in time through pressure to best the other swimmer. It is important to remind swimmers that they "strive *with*" their opponents—implying cooperative effort that results in important improvement for each competitor. Healthy attitudes toward competition are vital to athletic development. A second purpose for swim meets is to serve as a testing ground. During practice swimmers learn new techniques in strokes, starts, and turns, and meets are their opportunity to put those new skills to the test.

A third purpose of swim meets is providing an opportunity for young athletes to learn to compete with grace and sportsmanship, accepting all results with good behavior and learning to analyze their efforts for performance clues that will help in the future. The emotions of swim meets test swimmers, parents, and coaches. They are a great setting to learn about oneself and gain greater self-control.

Fourth, swim meets are fun! They can be social occasions as well as competitive ones, a celebration of fitness, good health, and youthful exuberance. Team spirit, cheering for fellow swimmers, and the excitement of seeing friends succeed in their efforts culminate in an exciting atmosphere.

Finally, swim meets are for the swimmers. Coaches, parents, and officials need always to remember that the swimmers have center stage at the meet. It's not about winning necessarily, or how well the coach has done, but about how each child meets the challenge and learns from it. Especially at the entry level of the sport, we must remember to be "athlete centered." Both coaches and officials must be continually sensitive to how their words, actions, and decisions affect the athletes in their care.

## Common Meet Procedures

As coach, it is vital that you understand how a meet is operated. Your responsibilities begin with properly entering your swimmers and getting them to their events on time. Then you observe their swims, critique their performances, and obtain their results. Many volunteer coaches will be responsible for hosting a meet or meets. When you do, you'll need to understand how to operate the meet, and you'll need help to do it.

Various mechanics are involved in operating any swim meet:

- Setting up the facility
- Providing meet information to visiting teams
- Entering swimmers in the proper events
- Organizing swimmers in heats for each event
- Starting and officiating the races
- Timing and compiling the results of each swim
- Keeping scores by team (if that is a part of the meet)

Next we'll discuss how you fit your team into this system. Here are the methods commonly used to accomplish each task.

### Setting Up the Facility

The pool manager and staff are usually responsible for pool set-up for a swim meet.

Designated areas for the competing teams should be separate from the spectators. Before the meet starts, lane markers or dividers, backstroke flags, and, if the water depth is appropriate, starting blocks should be in place (see Figure 6.2). If the starting blocks are over less than 5 feet of water, request that all races start from the water to reduce the chance of serious back and neck injury. Also check that the sound system is working properly to allow for communication during the meet.

**Figure 6.2** Lane markers should be in place before a meet starts.

### Providing Meet Information

As a meet host, you must provide meet logistics. All teams invited to your meet will want to know the following information: Where is the meet? Be sure to provide visiting teams with directions to the pool. When does warm-up start? When does the meet start? How many teams will be competing? What is the scoring system, and how will the meet be timed? How many swimmers from each team may compete in each event? Which events will be swum? A swim meet will proceed much smoother if teams have the answers to these questions before they arrive.

### Entering Swimmers in Events

Meets are either "deck-entered" or "pre-entered." In deck-entered meets, you typically complete one entry card per swimmer per event and give it to a "clerk of course" who organizes each event. In pre-entered meets,

you typically provide the host club with a sheet listing all swimmers' entries (sometimes accompanied with event cards), but other times you simply indicate to enter swimmers or provide previous best times so swimmers can be "seeded."

In any case, the system will usually be in place for you, and you simply need to clearly understand what you as coach must do to enter swimmers.

### Organizing Swimmers in Heats

If more swimmers have been entered in an event than there are lanes in the pool, several "heats" will take place. The times from all the heats are then compared to determine a winner. The clerk of course performs this duty. You will need to know where the clerk is located at the meet site and make sure you get your swimmers to that spot on time for each event. With novice teams this can be a major challenge! Once swimmers are at the clerk, the meet hosts organize the heats (by one of a variety of means, depending on both rules and local tradition). Some meets are "pyramid seeded," which means that the fastest swimmers are spread among the top three (or in some cases all) heats. Other meets are seeded with all the fastest swimmers in the last heat of the event. Some leagues have their own specific ways of placing swimmers in heats. Be sure to find out what method will be used in the meet your team is attending.

### Starting and Officiating the Races

Once swimmers are organized in heats, they compete one heat at a time. Officials (sometimes one, frequently more) conduct the meet, starting each race and judging each swim for conformity to the rules. These volunteer officials go through specific training programs to obtain their positions. Races are typically started with either an electric horn or a starter's pistol. Your swimmers will need to be familiar with the sound of each starting mechanism and know which mechanism will be used at each meet.

### Timing and Compiling the Results

Most novice meets are hand timed, with volunteers using stopwatches to record the

time of each competitor. The times are re-
corded on swimmers' event cards and are
sent to the scorers' table. Once results are
with the clerk, they are compiled, either
manually by sorting cards from fastest to
slowest or automatically by a computer con-
nected to the timing device. Compiled results
are then posted for everyone to see. Many
events, even in summer leagues, are now
electronically timed, which saves a great deal
of time and energy and is impartial among
competitors.

### Tabulating Team Scores

Team scores are handled in a similar manner—either hand tabulated or calculated by
computer and periodically posted and an-
nounced. The computer has become such a
prominent part of the swimming world that
much of the tedium of recording and report-
ing is now obsolete, and the scorers' office
has a much easier task.

## Officiating and Coaching

Coaches are responsible for the behavior and
control of their teams at a meet, and officials
are responsible for fair meets and competitive experiences. Coaches and officials must
work together closely and harmoniously for
meets to work smoothly for athletes and
spectators. Both leaders play such important roles that some special notes should be
made concerning each.

Swimming has a long-held tradition of
utmost courtesy between volunteer officials
and coaches. Both will make occasional mistakes in the course of a swim meet, and both
make some allowances for this human error
in the other. Unfailing politeness is expected;
in swimming, it is a very serious breach of
etiquette for either a coach or an official to
confront the other angrily.

When an official makes a particular call—
for example, a disqualification—it is acceptable practice for the coach to question the
head official to understand why the call was
made. But it is not acceptable for the coach
to dispute the call. Officials make calls based
on knowledge and experience, and coaches
may only inquire as to what the calls are.

Officials should never be coaching during
a meet (or showing visible enthusiasm for
any swimmer, even their own child), and
coaches should never be officiating. The two
roles do not mix. The responsibility of the
official is to conduct a fair competition, including disqualifications as necessary. Officials do not make corrections to swimmers—
that is the role of the coach.

## Your Team at a Swim Meet

As a coach, you have specific responsibilities
at a swim meet. First, you must ensure that
your team is properly entered. This administrative duty is not ever as simple as it sounds,
and it leads to much displeasure if not properly attended to. Check several times that all
swimmers are entered in the events you and
they wish to be in.

You must also make sure that transporta-
tion to and from the meet is covered. For
away meets you may need to hire a bus or
organize carpooling among parents.

At the meet site you must organize your
team and prepare them for their events.
There will be a warm-up time, and in most
cases a prepared warm-up schedule and
plan (see Figure 6.3). Adhere to it. If there is
no overall warm-up plan for swimmers, have
one preplanned for your own team, keeping
in mind that novice swimmers need 10 to 15

**Figure 6.3** Have a warm-up plan for your swimmers to use at meets.

minutes of warm-up and skill and drill practice.

Safety is a key concern in a crowded warm-up pool. The wise coach simulates this situation in advance, placing a large group of swimmers in one or two lanes at practice. Your team, especially those who are first-time meet swimmers, will be thankful for the rehearsal. Insist that your swimmers never dive into a crowded warm-up pool. If you attend a meet that has no established warm-up procedure, insist that one be developed.

Once it is time for the meet to begin, you'll need to make sure your swimmers get to the clerk on time. A buddy system can work well for first-timers, pairing experienced athletes with new ones to show them the ropes. Have a quick word with each swimmer before he or she competes to offer encouragement or a reminder of technique. You'll want to observe each swimmer's race. Doing team cheers before every swim is fun, but someone else should be organizing them so you can focus on the swimmers.

Each swimmer should return for your comments when her or his race is over. The compliment sandwich technique is a good one: Offer a bit of praise, then a bit of advice, then conclude with praise. "Brendan, you really swam well; I particularly liked your start. Maybe next time you can remember to keep your legs together when you kick butterfly. Your finish was well done also—your hands touched together. I'm glad you remembered that. Nice job—now get ready for your next swim."

You may want to have someone work with you to keep track of finishing places, pick up ribbons and awards for later distribution, and keep track of team scores. Your attention should be focused as much as possible on each individual athlete. But do remember to retain control of your team during the course of the meet; otherwise youngsters with long intervals between races may get bored and find something "entertaining" to do that might reflect badly on your team.

At the end of the meet, celebrate your participation with a team cheer, and make a point of thanking the meet hosts and officials. Make sure every team member has a safe way to get home. After attending to any remaining administrative duties, you can leave with a real sense of accomplishment.

## Swimming Terms to Know

Swimming has it own vocabulary. Becoming familiar with common swimming terms will make your job easier.

**aerobic training**—Training that uses oxygen to produce energy and during which no fatiguing lactate is produced by the body; easier, typically longer swims.

**age groups**—The typical division of swimmers into categories ( 8 and under, 9 and 10, 11 and 12, 13 and 14, etc.).

**bull-pen**—The location of the clerk of course, where swimmers congregate to be grouped into heats.

**circle seeding**—A method of grouping swimmers in heats that provides good competition for each athlete.

**circle swimming**—A method for letting multiple swimmers use each lane; in sequence, all swimmers swim up one side of the lane and swim back on the opposite side.

**classification**—A division of swimmers. Meets are typically organized by swimmer speed (C meets, B meets, A meets, AA meets, etc.).

**clerk of course**—The person who sets up meet races in order of the speed of competitors and from whom swimmers pick up their race cards.

**course**—The swimming length for a meet; can be long course (50 meters), or short course (25 meters or 25 yards).

**deck seeding**—A method of grouping swimmers into heats at a meet on the pool deck rather than beforehand.

**disqualification**—A violation of race rules.

**dual meet**—A competition between two teams.

**final**—A race held among the fastest six or eight swimmers after preliminary heats are held among all swimmers.

**flags**—Pennants hung above the water 5 meters from the wall to alert backstrokers that they are approaching the turning point.

**gun lap**—The final lap of a distance race (signaled by the firing of a gun when the lead swimmer is 5 meters from beginning the last lap).

**heat**—One of two or more divisions of an event where there are more swimmers than lanes.

**IM**—individual medley event. Swimmer swims four strokes: butterfly, backstroke, breaststroke, and freestyle (in that order).

**interval training**—Training that uses adjustments of distances swum, rest intervals between swims, speed, and number of repetitions to create workout sets.

**invitational**—A competition among three or more teams.

**jump**—To start ahead of the official's signal; also known as a false start.

**kick set**—A series of swim lengths of kicking only.

**meet director**—The person in overall charge of a swim meet.

**negative split**—A swim where the second half of the race was swum faster than the first half.

**positive check-in**—A meet procedure in which swimmers must check their names off on a sheet to show that they are present and wish to swim in the event.

**pull set**—A series of swim lengths of pulling only, usually done with a pullbuoy between the legs.

**ready room**—A location where swimmers are required to be before a final.

**recall rope**—The device, placed halfway down the pool, used to let swimmers know to return to the start after a false start.

**scratch**—To withdraw from an event.

**speed set**—A series of very short (12- to 25-yard) swims at high velocity.

**trials and finals**—A meet where initially all swimmers compete in the trials (also known as preliminaries) and then the fastest six or eight compete in the finals; usually a championship meet format only.

# UNIT 7

# What Swimming Skills and Drills Should I Teach?

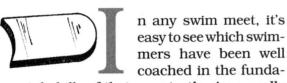

In any swim meet, it's easy to see which swimmers have been well coached in the fundamental skills of their sport—they're usually the ones out in front! In almost no other sport do teaching skills play such a primary role in the success of the athlete and the team. Good coaching will provide important competitive benefits, as well as deep and lasting personal satisfaction in teaching skills that can literally protect a life in the years to come.

In Unit 4 you learned how to teach skills and plan practices. This unit introduces you to the basic skills and techniques of swimming and provides drills and teaching ideas that will help you make swimming a lifetime sport for your athletes. Swimming skills are like an onion—there is always another layer.

Four basic strokes are involved in competitive swimming: freestyle (also called the crawl), backstroke, breaststroke, and butterfly. There are also two skills that swimmers must learn and perform consistently—starting and turning. Unit 7 presents the basic skills and drills for learning and performing these strokes and skills.

As you progress in your coaching career, you will discover much more to teach in each skill area. ASEP and the American Swimming Coaches Association provide extensive materials in every area.

## Teaching the Strokes

Use the same method to teach all the strokes. First introduce the stroke, and have an athlete with good skills demonstrate it several times. It can be helpful to do the demonstration first slowly, then at "race pace" (fast). Have the athletes view the stroke from different angles, including from poolside and underwater with goggles on, to help get a mental picture.

Next arrange the group in three or four rows, offer instruction on a particular part of the stroke (such as breathing, underwater pull, recovery, or kick), and then have athletes swim the next width or length, one row at a time, concentrating on that part. To create the verbal shorthand necessary for good teaching and learning, always use the same language and verbal cues. For example, you might have swimmers hold onto the edge of the pool and move through the kicking action following your verbal command, then move through the kick to establish their own rhythm.

Stroke drills are a way to isolate problem areas and concentrate on correcting them. Depending on your athletes' skill level, the time of the season, and the severity of the error, you'll need to vary the number and length of the drills you use. Typically, swimmers will swim a length or a width (25 yards) for a drill with repeated feedback from you. One drill especially useful for isolating skills is the "one-arm drill," which helps athletes concentrate on one part of the stroke.

Always finish each instructional period with a "whole-stroke swim" to remind swimmers what the purpose of the drill was and to provide the opportunity to put the entire stroke together.

## Freestyle

Freestyle is the fastest stroke, and most swim meets have more freestyle events and relays than any other. Good teaching for the freestyle will provide a solid start to your instructional program.

### Freestyle at a Glance

During the freestyle, the swimmer is face-down in the water. The arms move alternately, with one reaching in front of the shoulder and pulling through the water below the body as the other recovers over the water to the starting position. This cycle should be steady and smooth for greatest efficiency. The legs perform the flutter kick, providing a continuous balancing action for the body and arms. Streamlining is promoted by swimming predominantly on the side of the body, presenting as narrow an exposure as possible to the oncoming water.

### KEY TEACHING POINTS
### FOR FREESTYLE

**1. Hand entry:** The hand enters on a line in front of the shoulder and pitched slightly outward (see Figure 7.1).

***Verbal cue:*** "Extend and reach to enter the water."

**Figure 7.1**  In freestyle the hand enters on a line in front of the shoulder.

**2. Catch:** After extending the arm, the swimmer points the elbow toward the side of the pool and sweeps the hand outward, downward, and then upward toward the chest.

*Verbal cue:* "Reach over the barrel, elbow high."

**3. Pull:** The hand pulls under the body, with the elbow bent 90 degrees and pointing to the side wall (see Figure 7.2).

*Verbal cue:* "Pull under the body, elbow bent."

**Figure 7.2** In freestyle the hand pulls under the body, with the elbow bent at a 90-degree angle and pointing to the side wall.

**4. Armstroke finish:** The arm pulls through the water until the hand extends near the hip. The thumb touches the thigh, and the hand spins out of the water, little finger first (see Figure 7.3).

*Verbal cue:* "Thumb the thigh."

**Figure 7.3** In the freestyle armstroke finish the thumb touches the thigh, and the hand spins out of the water, little finger first.

**5. Recovery:** The recovery begins when the hand leaves the water near the thigh. The arm recovers with the elbow high and bent, the hand low and near the body. The arm should be relaxed (see Figure 7.4, a and b).

*Verbal cue:* "Hand close to the body and close to the water."

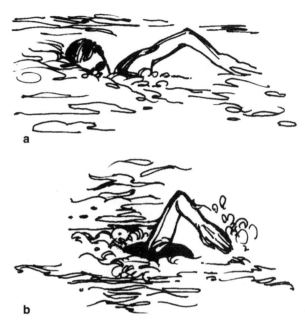

a

b

**Figure 7.4** Freestyle recovery phase: (a) the arm recovers with the elbow high and bent and with the hand low and near the body; (b) the arm should be relaxed.

**6. Kick:** Kicks will vary. The kick is steady, typically six beats per arm cycle, with ankles relaxed and toes pointed. The knees are slightly bent. The kick provides little propulsion; its role is to provide balance for the body and arm action.

*Verbal cue:* "Kick fast and steady."

**7. Breathing:** The head is held with the waterline approximately at the hairline (above the forehead). Looking forward and somewhat down, the swimmer should breathe continuously, exhaling underwater and inhaling by turning the head. By rolling the body to the side on which she or he will breathe, the swimmer should not need to turn the head much. The swimmer should begin turning the head before completing the arm pull to avoid breathing late (see Figure 7.5).

**Verbal cue:**   "Hide your breathing."

**Figure 7.5** In the freestyle the swimmer should begin turning the head before completing the arm pull to avoid breathing late.

## Freestyle Drills

*Name:* **The Scooter**

*Purpose:* To help the athlete learn to continue kicking while also pulling; as an alternative emphasis, the drill will help the swimmer learn the correct arm motion by isolating the action.

*Organization:* Have the swimmer extend one arm over a kickboard, keeping the face in the water and using the other arm to pull. The

---

## Error Detection and Correction for Freestyle

| ERROR | CORRECTION |
|---|---|
| 1. The swimmer "wiggles" down the pool, with hips moving from side to side. | 1. The swimmer needs to work on the hand entry. Make sure the hands enter at the shoulder line and do not cross over in front of the head. A fast, steady kick will help keep the body from wiggling. |
| 2. The swimmer takes many strokes but makes little progress. | 2. The arm pull should have three dimensions—length, width, and depth. Length is achieved by extending the arm fully in front of the shoulder and pulling through to the thigh. The stroke has width if the swimmer pulls out slightly and back under the body before thumbing the thigh. The arm should reach maximum depth bent 90 degrees at the elbow. Remind swimmers that arms provide the propulsion and legs the balance. These swimmers will not fatigue as quickly once the kick is de-emphasized. |
| 3. Arm recovery is wild. | 3. Have the athlete swim directly next to the wall. The hand and arm must be in the correct position or the swimmer will hit the hand into the wall. Use the fingertip drill with the elbow up to increase the swimmer's awareness of where both the hand and the water are. |
| 4. The swimmer swims with the head completely underwater. | 4. The swimmer must work to adjust the head position so that the water hits at about the hairline. The swimmer should be looking slightly forward and down. Lifting the head will improve body position, making the body more streamlined and allowing the water to move over it with no drag or resistance. |

swimmer should breathe on the side of the pulling arm. More advanced swimmers can work without the kickboard, extending one arm and pulling with the other. Swimmers should swim one length or width at a time.

*Coaching points:* Remind swimmers to keep the legs kicking continuously while pulling. Remember to have them do the drill with both arms.

*Name:* **Kicking Drill**

*Purpose:* To strengthen the legs.

*Organization:* This drill can be done with or without a kickboard. The swimmer should perform the drill primarily on the side (the predominant body position the freestyle is swum in). The emphasis is a fast, steady kick. Have swimmers count the rhythm in their heads: "1, 2, 3, 4, 5, 6." Swimmers should alternate having their hands in front and at the sides. When swimming on the side, the swimmer should extend the arm on the bottom over the head and put the surface arm by the side.

*Coaching points:* Make sure swimmers keep their ankles loose, flexible, and relaxed.

*Name:* **Zipper and Fingertip Drill**

*Purpose:* To teach the swimmer to keep the hand close to the body during the recovery.

*Organization:* While swimming the freestyle, the swimmer "drags" the recovery hand all the way up the side of the body, with the thumb touching the side all the way to the armpit before extending to the front entry position. This helps get the elbow up high on the recovery. As a variation, the swimmer no longer drags the thumb along the body but drags the fingertips through the water, keeping the elbow high. The swimmer should perform one to two lengths before resting and moving on to the next drill.

*Coaching points:* Keep the elbow high, directly over the hand. Keep the hand, wrist, and arm relaxed.

*Name:* **Body Roll Drill**

*Purpose:* To teach the swimmer to roll the body from side to side during the freestyle.

*Organization:* The swimmer pushes off the wall in a streamlined position. Swimming on the side, the bottom arm extended and the top arm along the side, the swimmer kicks six times and pulls the arm through half a cycle until on the other side, kicks six more times and repeats the arm pull, and so on. The drill should be swum for 25 to 50 yards.

*Coaching points:* Cue swimmers that their navels should face the side wall of the pool and to allow the hips to turn the entire body.

*Name:* **Double Recovery Drill**

*Purpose:* To teach the swimmer to keep the recovery arm close to the body and close to the water.

*Organization:* With one hand at a time, the swimmer touches the water at the correct entry point, reverses the pattern of the recovery hand until it "thumbs the thigh" once again, then moves it forward again to enter and begin the next pull. This ingrains the hand pattern on the recovery. The athlete should swim one or two lengths at a time.

*Coaching point:* Tell swimmers to keep the hand in view during the recovery.

## Backstroke

Backstroke is one of the oldest of the strokes, and it has seen much change in the past two decades. Speeds have increased rapidly with the emergence of better pulling techniques. To coach the backstroke effectively, concentrate on teaching a strong kick and a "still head."

### Backstroke at a Glance

The swimmer keeps the head still and the body lined up behind the shoulders. The body rolls from side to side, but the head remains still and the eyes are focused upward. The arms alternate and make a deep catch on the water, with rapid arm recovery.

### KEY TEACHING POINTS FOR BACKSTROKE

**1. Hand entry:** With the head being at 12 o'clock, the hands enter the water at 11 and 1 o'clock, with the little finger entering the water first and the palm turned outward (see

Figure 7.6). The hands enter the water like a knife.

***Verbal cue:*** "Hand enters little finger first."

**Figure 7.6** In the backstroke the head is at 12 o'clock, and the hands enter the water at 11 o'clock and 1 o'clock, with the little finger entering the water first and the palm turned outward.

**2. Catch:** The hand drives down deep into the water, with the arm remaining straight (see Figure 7.7).

***Verbal cue:*** "Drive the hand deep."

**Figure 7.7** During the catch phase of the backstroke, the hand drives down deep into the water first, with the arm remaining straight.

**3. Pull:** Once the hand is deep, the elbow bends. It continues to bend until it reaches 90 degrees, about halfway through the pull. The hand comes up and over as the arm

begins to extend. It sweeps up and out past the hip (see Figure 7.8).

***Verbal cue:*** "Up and over, then sweep out past hip."

**Figure 7.8** Once the hand is deep on the backstroke pull, the elbow bends until it reaches 90°, about halfway through the pull.

**4. Finish:** The hand exits thumb first, next to the hip, moving last into an upward arc (see Figure 7.9). The swimmer should concentrate on accelerating through the pull, with no pause as the hand leaves the water.

***Verbal cue:*** "Thumb first, accelerate out."

**Figure 7.9** On the backstroke finish the hand exits, thumb first, next to the hip, moving last into an upward arc.

**5. Arm recovery:** The elbow is fully extended as the arm leaves the water. It continues with no bend in the elbow as the arm recovers directly over the shoulder. The shoulder rolls up and out of the water. The hand is rotated so the little finger leads the recovery and enters the water first (see Figure 7.10).

***Verbal cue:*** "Little finger leads."

## Error Detection and Correction for the Backstroke

| ERROR | CORRECTION |
|---|---|
| 1. The swimmer wiggles from side to side and has wild arm action. | 1. Check the head position. It must be very still, never moving. If the swimmer keeps the eyes still, the head will follow. Also make sure the swimmer's arms are recovering straight over the body and that the hands are entering the water at 11 and 1 o'clock. |
| 2. The swimmer is "flat," with both shoulders in the water at the same time, creating resistance. | 2. Have the swimmer add a body roll, lifting one shoulder out when the other hand goes deep and rotating on the long axis. One-arm drills will also help work the other shoulder up and out. Also have the swimmer work on the backstroke kick with the head up and the body turned on the side. |
| 3. The swimmer is "sitting down" in the water with the feet low. | 3. The swimmer must get the head back and still, kick rapidly, and lift the hips toward the water surface. |

**Figure 7.10** In the backstroke the elbow is fully extended as the arm leaves the water, recovering over the shoulder with no bend.

**6. Kick:** The swimmer uses the flutter kick in backstroke. The kick is fast and powerful, six beats per arm cycle, and deeper than the freestyle kick. As in freestyle, the kick is similar to kicking a ball: The leg is straight as it moves downward, and the knee bends as it moves upward. The toes are pointed.

*Verbal cue:* "Fast and deep."

**7. Body position:** The head is high and never moves, and the eyes look up. The swimmer should concentrate on keeping the hips high; there is no "sitting" or bending. The body rotates on the long axis, from side to side. (See Figure 7.11.)

*Verbal cue:* "Backstroke swum on the side."

**8. Breathing:** Inhale on one hand entry, exhale on the next.

*Verbal cue:* "Inhale, pull; exhale, pull" or "inhale, right; exhale, left."

**Figure 7.11** In the backstroke the body rotates on the long axis, from side to side.

## Backstroke Drills

*Name:* **Kicking Drill**

*Purpose:* To teach the swimmer correct kicking techniques and proper head and hip position.

*Organization:* The swimmer pushes off the wall, swimming on the back. The arms are extended overhead, the body in a streamlined position. The swimmer kicks the length of the pool, keeping the toes pointed and allowing the knees to bend somewhat. This drill becomes a conditioning drill if repeated for a number of lengths.

*Name:* **One-Arm Backstroke Drill**

*Purpose:* To isolate the correct action of each arm.

*Organization:* Using one arm at a time to work on each phase of the pull and recovery, the swimmer places the nonworking hand at the side of the body (not overhead) so that the body can roll. The athlete swims one length or width at a time, alternating arms. The drill can be repeated with the swimmer focusing on a different phase of the pull each time.

*Coaching point:* Remind swimmers to drive the entry hand deep before beginning the pull.

*Name:* **Quarter Drill**

*Purpose:* To encourage the swimmer to keep the head still during the backstroke.

*Organization:* The swimmer places a quarter flat on the forehead then swims the length or width of the pool without losing it.

*Coaching point:* This drill is more challenging than it sounds—make sure swimmers use a normal armstroke pattern.

*Name:* **Spin Drill**

*Purpose:* To increase stroke turnover.

*Organization:* The swimmer should lift the head high, look at the other end of the pool, "sit down" in the water with the hips, and rotate the arms as fast as possible. This helps swimmers learn how to increase stroke turnover, but because the body position in this drill is not desirable for correct technique, swimmers should perform the drill only infrequently. One or two lengths is appropriate.

*Coaching point:* Encourage swimmers to keep a very high stroke rate and hand acceleration during the pull.

# Breaststroke

The breaststroke, the slowest of the four competitive strokes, requires the most pure power. It is the oldest known swimming stroke, and there have been many changes over the past 20 years. The stroke also has the greatest variation of successful techniques; the arm and leg actions and timing can tolerate a great deal of individual adaptation to limb sizes and personal strengths. Allow swimmers some latitude in how they swim the breaststroke.

## Breaststroke at a Glance

In the breaststroke, the arms and legs alternate action. The stroke begins with the arm pull, then the legs kick as the arms recover to the beginning position. In the third and final phase, the arms extend fully overhead briefly in a stretch position before beginning the next pull. The rules require that the body remain horizontal and that the arms pull simultaneously. The legs must also kick simultaneously. All the action of the limbs is underwater. The rules also require that the head break the surface of the water once each stroke cycle.

### KEY TEACHING POINTS
### FOR BREASTSTROKE

**1. Pull:** The swimmer is prone in the water with the arms extended overhead. The eyes look at the hands, which are several inches underwater. The palms are turned outward, forming a *V* with the backs of the hands. The palms are then pressed outward until they are positioned wider than the elbows (see Figure 7.12). The swimmer turns the hands down but keeps the elbows up, rotates the forearms and the hands under the elbows, then accelerates the hands "outside to center" and squeezes the elbows together. The swimmer should not pull past the shoulder line.

*Verbal cue:* "Press wide, pitch hands up, turn fingers down, and squeeze."

**Figure 7.12** In the breaststroke pull the palms of the hands are turned and pressed outward until they are wider apart than the elbows.

**2. Kick:** The swimmer begins the kick face-down with the legs extended and toes pointed. The heels are lifted to the surface, and as the feet near the buttocks, the toes are rotated outward (see Figure 7.13, a and b). The swimmer then kicks out, back, down, and around, in a smooth accelerating motion, "squeezing" the back of the kick by pressing the ankles together. The legs should be fully extended and ready for the next kick.

*Verbal cue:* "Kick out, back, down, and around; squeeze the ankles together."

**3. Timing:** Swimmers should pull, keeping the legs streamlined, then kick as the arms recover to a streamlined position. There should be a brief stretch as the entire body is streamlined before the next pull begins. The three phases of the stroke will become less isolated as the swimmer gains experience and swims faster.

*Verbal cue:* "Kick, stretch, pull."

**4. Breathing:** The swimmer should breathe on each stroke. The swimmer begins the arm pull, lifts the head while pulling, and inhales as the hands are coming together in the center. The swimmer then returns the head to the water while completing the kick. This technique lets swimmers breathe at the "high point" of the stroke. To find the high point, athletes should swim the stroke with the

head in the water and feel where in the stroke cycle the body is naturally the highest.

*Verbal cue:* "Breathe at the high point of the stroke."

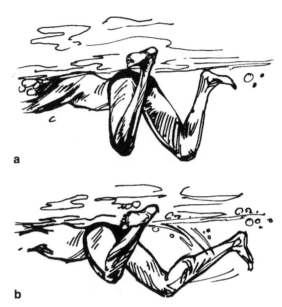

**Figure 7.13** The breaststroke kick: (a) the toes are pointed and the heels lifted to the surface. As the feet near the buttocks, the toes rotate outward; (b) the kicking motion is out, back, down, and around.

### *Breaststroke Drills*

*Name:* **Kicking Drill**

*Purpose:* To develop leg strength and to practice kicking.

*Organization:* The swimmer can perform this drill with or without a kickboard, and even with more than one kickboard to help get the proper kicking depth. Without the kickboard, the swimmer should do some kicking with the hands locked together in front of the body and also with the hands back at the hips. Bring the heels up and kick the fingers. The swimmer can also place hands to the side and touch the heels with each kick. Swimmers can do one or more lengths of each variation of the drill. The shorter the distance, the more the swimmer can focus on technique.

*Coaching point:* Emphasize that swimmers complete the kick by whipping the legs around and consciously bringing the ankles together.

*Name:* **Timing Drill**

*Purpose:* To ensure correct timing on the interaction between kicking and pulling.

*Organization:* Swimmers should perform one pull and two kicks, then one pull and three kicks, then reduce to "kick, stretch, pull; kick, stretch, pull." Experiment with having swimmers hold the stretch phase for 1, 2, and 3 counts. Have them repeat the sequence until the entire distance is complete. This drill can be swum one or two lengths at a time.

*Coaching point:* Emphasize the separation of the kick and the pull, then gradually allow the two to come closer together.

*Name:* **Squeeze Drill**

*Purpose:* To get the upper body clear of the water before the force of the kick is applied.

*Organization:* Using a pullbuoy, the swimmer concentrates on squeezing the elbows together hard under the shoulders to lift the upper body clear of water.

*Coaching point:* Remind swimmers to get their shoulders out of the water.

*Name:* **Breaststroke Kick on Back Drill**

*Purpose:* To emphasize the depth dimension of the kick.

*Organization:* Have swimmer turn over onto the back. With hands at sides, swimmer kicks backward with a breaststroke action. Emphasize that the heels lift to the hands before the kick back.

*Coaching point:* Swimmers must kick all the way through (finish the kick) until the legs are straight.

---

## Error Detection and Correction for Breaststroke

| ERROR | CORRECTION |
|---|---|
| 1. The swimmer kicks but does not move forward. | 1. Check for the three-dimensional kick—back, down, and around. Look for flexed, not extended, feet and check for acceleration of the legs during the kick. Also check that the swimmer is bringing the heels to the buttocks (as opposed to pulling the knees under the body). |
| 2. The swimmer pulls but does not move forward. | 2. Check the following elements in order: The palms should face out; the hands should be pressed wider than the elbows; the hands should be rotated down and sweep into the center line of the body; and the hands should accelerate from wide to center. |
| 3. The swimmer kicks and pulls at the same time. | 3. Emphasize a slow-motion breaststroke—pull, kick, stretch. Also emphasize the glide. |
| 4. The swimmer can only turn the toes out on one foot; the other toes point inward. | 4. Hold the swimmer's feet in proper position in the water and let the swimmer push off your hands until she or he gets to feel the pressure on the instep of the foot. Or have the swimmer lay on top of a kickboard and practice kicking. This will require the swimmer's hips to remain flat in the water. Correcting this error may take a lot of patience and repetition. |

*Name:* **Pulling Drill**

*Purpose:* To develop upper body strength.

*Organization:* This drill can be done with or without a pullbuoy. With the pullbuoy, the swimmer works on pressing the hand wide and pitching the little finger upward to the surface. Without the pullbuoy, the swimmer emphasizes lifting the hips to the surface as the hands stretch forward. Because this drill is slow, it can be frustrating for beginning swimmers. More advanced swimmers can pull one or more lengths for a conditioning exercise.

*Coaching point:* Have swimmers accelerate the hands on the in sweep.

## Butterfly

The newest of the four competitive strokes, the butterfly is the second fastest. Novice swimmers may perceive the butterfly as the most difficult stroke to swim, but this is not true if it is taught as a body and a rhythm stroke rather than a kick-dominated stroke. You should emphasize using the roll motion of the body to keep the stroke moving forward.

### Butterfly at a Glance

The butterfly is a rhythmic stroke, with arms and legs acting together. The swimmer is prone in the water and must keep the body horizontal. The arms pull simultaneously underwater and recover over the surface simultaneously. The legs kick up and down simultaneously, using a dolphinlike action with significant knee bend. When the butterfly is properly executed, it looks like the swimmer is "rolling through water."

#### KEY TEACHING POINTS FOR BUTTERFLY

**1. Body position:** The butterfly is a body stroke. The body rolls through the water, alternating hips high and chest down (see Figure 7.14) with hips down and chest high. This motion creates a "teeter-totter" effect of the body, with the legs following the hip action. Swimmers should concentrate on allowing the hips to move up and down

significantly. Emphasize that the kick originates from the hips, not from the legs and feet.

**Verbal cue:** "Press chest down, hips up."

**Figure 7.14**　In the butterfly the body rolls through the water, alternating hips high and chest down with hips down and chest high.

**2. Kick:** The kick begins with the legs extended and the toes pointed. The legs are lifted upward, with the knees straight; the knees bend as the feet whip downward. The downward thrust of the kick will cause the hips to rise, creating the undulating motion.

**Verbal cue:** Don't use one; deemphasize the legs when teaching the butterfly.

**3. Arm pull:** The hands enter the water slightly wider than the shoulders; the thumbs go in first, sweep out, move in under the throat, and press back and out past the hips (see Figure 7.15). The elbows are bent about 90 degrees at their maximum under the throat or upper chest.

**Verbal cue:** "Sweep in, sweep out."

**4. Arm recovery:** The hands recover over the water with the little finger leading (see

**Figure 7.15**　During the butterfly arm pull the hands enter the water slightly wider than the shoulders; the thumbs go in first, sweep out, and then move in under the throat.

Figure 7.16). The elbows are straight and the arms should remain low.

***Verbal cue:*** "Hand recovers with little finger leading."

**Figure 7.16**    In the butterfly the hands recover over the water with the little finger leading, the elbows straight, and the arms low.

**5. Timing:** The hands go in as the hips go up (see Figure 7.17)—this sentence captures

**Figure 7.17**    In the butterfly the hands go in as the hips go up.

the perfect timing of the kick with the armstroke.

***Verbal cue:*** "Hands in, hips up."

**6. Breathing:** The swimmer stretches the neck forward to inhale at the end of the arm pull before the hands exit the water (see Figure 7.18). The swimmer should be looking at the other end of the pool. The head is back in the water during the recovery phase of the stroke. To avoid holding the breath, the ath-

---

### *Error Detection and Correction for Butterfly*

| ERROR | CORRECTION |
|---|---|
| 1. The swimmer has poor timing between the kick and the pull. Often the body remains flat in the water, with little undulation. | 1. Emphasize the cue "as hands go in, hips go up." Use the one-arm fly drill to refine and tune this timing. |
| 2. The swimmer "overkicks" and tires quickly. | 2. Emphasize that this is a body roll stroke, not a kick stroke. Swimmers should focus on pulling through the water, not wide. The one-arm fly drill is very useful. |
| 3. The swimmer's head is up during the recovery. | 3. Emphasize exhalation of breath underwater during the entire arm pull, then a quick inhalation as the hands finish the pull. To time the head lift properly, the swimmer should use the "left arm, right arm, both arms" drill, breathing only on the both-arms segment. |
| 4. The swimmer has a stiff kick, with little knee bend. | 4. Cue the swimmer to relax at the knees and allow the downbeat of the kick to produce some bend. Emphasize two portions of the kick: an upbeat and a downbeat. The dolphin kick on back drill will help swimmers feel both portions of the kick, leading to greater knee bend on the downbeat. |

**Figure 7.18** Butterfly breathing phase: the swimmer stretches the neck forward to inhale at the end of the arm pull before the hands exit the water.

lete should begin to exhale at the beginning of the arm pull.

**Verbal cue:** "Stretch to breathe."

## Butterfly Drills

*Name:* **One-Arm Fly Drill**

*Purpose:* To teach correct stroke timing and promote concentration on the pulling pattern of each arm.

*Organization:* The swimmer performs the butterfly with only one arm, keeping the other arm out in front, concentrating on pushing the hips up when the hand enters the water. One length or width of the drill is performed with each arm. This drill helps swimmers relax during the butterfly and emphasizes each part of the entry, pull, and recovery.

*Coaching point:* Remind swimmers that "hands go in, hips go up."

*Name:* **"Left Arm, Right Arm, Both Arms" Drill**

*Purpose:* To help swimmers master performing the butterfly rhythm without excessive fatigue.

*Organization:* The swimmer pushes off the wall in a streamlined position, pulling and recovering with the right arm, then with the left arm, then with both arms. The nonpulling arm should remain extended in front. Use a variety of patterns (like "three left arm, three right arm, one double" or "two left, two right, two double"). This drill helps swimmers maintain good stroke posture and timing while doing a lot of butterfly. It is also effective in helping beginners put the entire stroke together.

*Coaching point:* Swimmers need to concentrate on the phrase "hands go in, hips go up."

*Name:* **Dolphin Kick on Back Drill**

*Purpose:* To emphasize both the up and down beats of the kick.

*Organization:* Swimmers perform the dolphin kick while on their backs, with hands at their sides or above the head. This drill teaches swimmers to kick both up and down. Have swimmers kick either one length or width as a drill or a number of lengths as a conditioning exercise.

*Coaching point:* Be sure to work the kick in both directions.

*Name:* **Nail the Entry Drill**

*Purpose:* To emphasize the head action.

*Organization:* The swimmer pretends the forehead is a hammer and "nails" it downward on the entry to prevent keeping the head up too long after taking the breath. Have swimmers do one or two lengths or widths.

*Coaching point:* Keep the head aligned with the spine.

*Name:* **Underwater Fly Drill**

*Purpose:* To promote concentration on the pull pattern.

*Organization:* The athlete swims the whole stroke but at the end of the pull recovers the hands forward under the chest and into the next pull, maintaining the body roll. Swimmers should do one or two lengths or widths.

*Coaching point:* The hands should be closest together under the throat during the pull.

In addition to the drills outlined in this unit are hundreds more geared to specific purposes. Many articles, books, and videos are available to help you find the right drill for the problems your swimmers face. Contact ASEP (800-747-5698) or the American Swimming Coaches Association (800-356-2722) for the appropriate resources for your needs.

## Teaching Swimming Starts

An important part of the swim race is the start. It is also one of the few situations in the sport with potential for serious injury. Make sure that there is at least 5 feet of water directly under the block where swimmers will be starting and the same amount of water for 15 feet out (it should not get shallower). If not, all races should be started from within the water. Safety is paramount!

Be especially careful when you teach racing starts to novices. It is preferable to use water at least 8 feet deep at first, then move to 5 feet when the athlete can successfully complete a shallow start in deep water 10 out of 10 times. The first time in 5 feet, have the swimmer execute the start from the deck before moving to the starting block. Then when a novice executes the first few starts from a block, be in the water in position to grab the swimmer if he or she loses control and appears to be falling into a steep entry angle. Practice this way until the swimmer can successfully complete a number of dives.

Be sure to remind swimmers to dive shallowly, and emphasize that the arms should be over the head on all forward starts. Not only does the swimmer enter the water in a streamlined position, but the arms will help break the impact if the swimmer does hit the bottom. A swimmer could be seriously injured, even paralyzed, by hitting the bottom with the head, neck, or back.

There are variations in the forward start to accommodate the specific needs of freestyle, breaststroke, and butterfly. Swimmers need to learn the backstroke start as well. Once again, having good demonstrators is very important. A good videotape is also an excellent teaching aid.

## The Forward Start

The same basic start is used for the freestyle, the breaststroke, and the butterfly. Once in the water, however, the swimmer executes slightly different movements.

At the starter's command of "take your mark," the swimmer assumes the following starting position for all three strokes (see Figure 7.19):

• The toes are over the edge of the starting block.

• The feet are shoulder-width apart.

**Figure 7.19** Position for the forward start: toes over the edge of the starting block, feet shoulder width apart, hips lined up over the heels, swimmer bent forward gripping the block with both hands, hands placed between the feet, and knees bent.

• The hips are lined up over the heels.

• The swimmer bends forward and grips the block with both hands, hands placed between the feet and knees bent.

• The eyes look down and slightly back.

At the starting signal (a gunshot or horn blast), the swimmer executes the following movements:

• At the signal the swimmer pulls down on the block with the hands, the head pops forward and up, and the eyes seek the entry spot (see Figure 7.20a).

• As the legs begin the drive to leap, the hands and arms stretch out and aim at the entry spot (see Figure 7.20, b and c).

• During the flight of the dive, the head is tucked down between the arms, which remain extended.

• The swimmer imagines entering the water through one "hole."

• The hands are adjusted to provide a shallow dive angle as soon as they enter the water.

### Start Variations by Stroke

**Freestyle:** The swimmer stretches underwater, streamlines, and when feeling the

As speed diminishes, the swimmer counts "1, 2, 3," then does a wide pull-out and push-through motion with the hands ending by the hips (see Figure 7.21, a-c). The swimmer counts "1, 2" before beginning the recovery with the hands under the body, palms up and elbows tucked in. As the hands pass the face on the way back to the front, the swimmer kicks once to the surface. Once the head breaks the surface, the swimmer begins the regular breaststroke and breathes on the first stroke.

**Butterfly:** The swimmer streamlines, then, as speed diminishes, takes two or three quick kicks and times the first armstroke to break smoothly through to the surface. The swimmer should complete one or more strokes before breathing.

**Figure 7.20** Start motion: at the signal (a) the swimmer pulls down on the block with the hands; (b) the head pops forward and up, and the eyes seek the entry spot; and (c) as the legs begin the drive to leap, the hands and arms stretch out and aim at entry spot.

speed diminish, starts to kick, then takes two pulls before the first breath.

**Breaststroke:** The swimmer streamlines, keeping the head tucked between the arms.

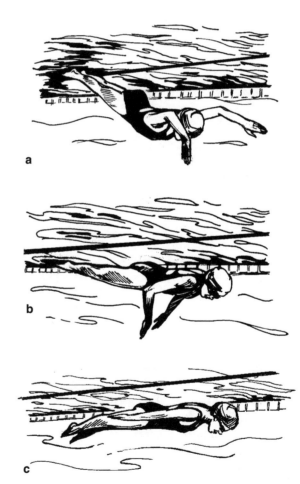

**Figure 7.21** Breaststroke start: (a) the swimmer streamlines, keeping the head tucked between the arms; counts "1,2,3;" and then does a wide pull-out; (b and c) the swimmer pushes through the motion with the hands ending by the hips.

## *The Backstroke Start*

The backstroke start is really a back dive, or leap, in which the swimmer arches the back out over the water. Young children will have a certain amount of fear associated with this motion at the outset; it's best to begin teaching the backstroke start by having swimmers practice the motion down in the water. Then gradually pull them up out of the water as their technique improves. This progression will help swimmers avoid the stinging "back smacks" that result from poor technique.

When the starter says "take your mark," the swimmer assumes the following starting position for the backstroke:

• Hands are on the backstroke bar on the starting block, palms down (see Figure 7.22a).

• Feet are against the wall about 1 foot underwater, either side by side or one slightly above the other (whichever is more comfort-

able). Depending on the rules, it may be okay for toes to be out of the water.

• The body is pulled up reasonably high out of the water, the head close to the block (see Figure 7.22b). At most, the buttocks will barely clear the surface of the water.

At the starting signal, the swimmer executes the following movements:

• The head snaps back (see Figure 7.22c).

• The hands push the body away from the bar (see Figure 7.22d).

• The legs drive the body up, out, and away from the wall in a back dive (see Figure 7.22d).

• The eyes look back over the shoulders (see Figure 7.22d).

• The arms sweep over the top and reach for the entry spot (see Figure 7.22e).

• The swimmer focuses on entering through one "hole" (see Figure 7.22e).

**Figure 7.22**   Backstroke starting position: (a) hands on the backstroke bar on the starting block, palms down; (b) feet placed about 1 foot underwater, body pulled out of the water, head close to the block. At the starting signal (c) the swimmer's head snaps back; (d) the hands push the body away from bar, and the legs drive the body up, out, and away from the wall in a back dive, the head looking back over the shoulders; (e) and the arms sweep over the top and reach for the entry spot.

Once in the water, the swimmer streamlines and glides until deceleration begins, then kicks using the dolphin or flutter kick and takes the first pull, which breaks the body through the surface.

## Relay Starts

In relays, the incoming swimmer must touch the wall before the outgoing swimmer's toes leave the starting block. Here are some teaching tips for the incoming swimmer (see Figure 7.23):

• Hold your breath for the last four strokes to the wall.

• Finish your leg with consistent stroke and rhythm.

• Kick hard to the wall.

• Touch the wall with fingertips and arm fully extended.

• Always stretch the last stroke, rather than "short stroke" to the wall.

**Figure 7.23**   In relays the incoming swimmer kicks hard to the wall and touches it with the fingertips, the arm fully extended. The outgoing swimmer begins the windup when the incoming swimmer is two strokes from the wall.

Here are some tips for the outgoing swimmer (see Figure 7.23):

• Use a windup start for momentum. Instead of grabbing the starting block, extend arms over the water.

• Begin the windup by swinging the arms up and around when the incoming swimmer is two strokes from the wall.

• Accelerate the windup and go fast when the incoming swimmer's shoulders cross the *T* on the bottom of the pool.

• Complete a full circle with the arms. As they swing forward, execute a normal dive. Do not go deeper or shallower or "lift the legs" on a relay start.

## Teaching Turns

A thorough explanation of how to teach the many turn techniques goes beyond the scope of this text. But what follows are the basic instructions for teaching turns to your swimmers. As with other skills, one of the best things you can do to teach turns is to enlist the help of an experienced swimmer to do a series of good demonstrations. A picture truly is worth a thousand words in teaching these skills.

## Freestyle Turn

Misnamed the "flip" turn, the freestyle turn is actually more like a twist or a shoulder roll. The swimmer should approach the wall, lower one shoulder, and "roll" on that shoulder, throwing the feet to the wall (see Figure 7.24). The swimmer's arms extend over the head into a streamlined position, with the back of the head tightly against the upper arms, and the swimmer pushes hard with the legs off the wall. As the body decelerates, the legs begin their kick, then the arms start with two strokes before the first breath.

**Figure 7.24**   In the freestyle turn the swimmer approaches the wall, lowers one shoulder, and "rolls" on that shoulder, throwing the feet to the wall.

## Backstroke Turn

Rules for the backstroke have recently changed to allow the swimmer to turn over to the stomach after the last stroke and execute a somersault, throwing the feet to the wall and pushing off on the back into a streamlined position. Again, the swimmer should kick first, then pull.

## Breaststroke Turn

The swimmer's hands must touch the wall at the same time (see Figure 7.25a). Approaching the wall, the swimmer kicks into the turn, with the arms extended (see Figure 7.25b). After the touch, one arm recovers under the water and the other arm over, near the swimmer's ear, as the swimmer positions on the side to push off the wall (see Figure 7.25c). The swimmer streamlines, then pushes off (see Figure 7.25d), holding the "1, 2, 3" count described for the pull-out following the start (see p. 57). The same sequence is followed after each breaststroke turn.

## Butterfly Turn

The swimmer's hands must touch the wall at the same time. The mechanics of the turn are the same as for the breaststroke, with the swimmer leaving the wall on the side, then executing two quick kicks and initiating the first pull. The swimmer should take one complete pull before the first breath to avoid coming up and breathing into the bow wave or turn wave of other swimmers.

## Individual Medley Turns

The individual medley, or IM, is a race that features all four strokes—starting with butterfly, then backstroke, breaststroke, and freestyle. Typical novice IM races are 100 yards. An easy place for your swimmers to gain an advantage in the IM is in the transition turns, which few novice swimmers execute well. Here are the points to teach your swimmers for each transition turn.

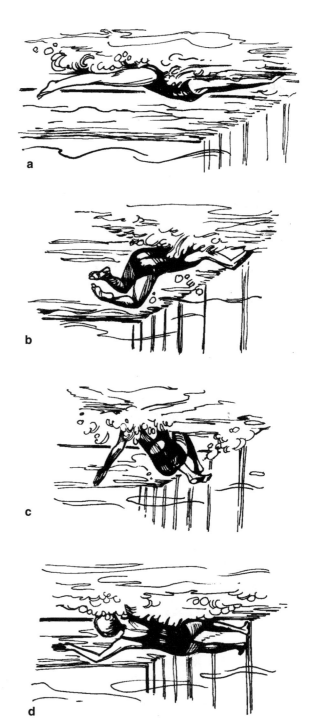

**Figure 7.25** Phases of the breaststroke turn: (a) two hands touch the wall at the same time; (b) feet swing toward the wall; (c) swimmer positions to push off the wall; and (d) swimmer streamlines, then pushes off.

### Butterfly to Backstroke

The swimmer executes a two-hand butterfly touch, then drops down onto the back, pushing off underwater to a streamlined back-stroke position.

### Back to Breast

There are numerous versions of this turn. The simplest is to execute a normal back-stroke finish, turning the head to one side while taking care not to turn the hips past the vertical line, and then to turn onto the side by the turned head and push off into a breaststroke pull-out from the side position. The touching hand recovers over the water and the hand in the water remains underwa-ter, assisting with the balance of the turn.

### Breast to Free

This turn is a simple execution of a two-hand breaststroke finish, followed by a half turn into a position on the side and a streamlined push off the wall.

Covering all the skills discussed in this unit in one season is a very ambitious goal with novice swimmers. Be cautious about creating overly enthusiastic plans. It is bet-ter that your swimmers know several skills extremely well, to the point of habit, than a vast array of skills only moderately well.

Unit 8 describes how to take the skill teaching you learned in this unit and use it to enhance your overall effort of building a strong swim team.

# UNIT 8

# *Building a Strong Swim Team*

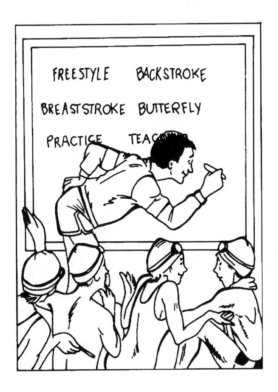

FREESTYLE  BACKSTROKE

BREASTSTROKE  BUTTERFLY

PRACTICE  TEAC...

The most important factors in doing quality coaching are attending to athletes and teaching appropriate skills and attitudes. When you develop your plan for your team, these factors come first. In this unit we'll touch on other considerations you'll want to take into account, including

- *developing all strokes,*

- *recognizing and developing individual talents,*

- *building the team aspects of swimming, and*

- *teaching athletes how to race in the pool.*

In a sport where the racing is quite straight-forward, these four aspects constitute coaching "strategies." By working on these four areas to the maximum, you'll be able to present a team that is exciting, fun to be part of, and competitively successful.

## Developing All Strokes

Every swimmer, even one who shows early ability in one stroke, should be encouraged to develop all four competitive strokes through intensive practice time and racing experience. In planning your season, you'll want to make sure that all swimmers have the opportunity to experience and develop each stroke. Don't make the mistake of deciding to swim mostly freestyle "because everyone can do it." It is better to design swimming sets that use shorter distances (25s or even widths) and coach all four strokes than to use overdistance swimming in freestyle only.

---

### A Short Repeat Practice Session

**Warm-up:** 10 × 25 alternate kick and swim on 45 seconds—freestyle.

**Teaching set:** 12 × 50 alternate 6 backstroke on 1:15 with 6 breaststroke. Use drills on the first 25, whole stroke on the second 25.

**Training set:** 6 × 75 (25 butterfly, 50 freestyle) on 2:00 with whole stroke butterfly and freestyle drills.

**Teaching set:** 20 × 12-1/2 (widths)— butterfly drills and whole stroke.

**Cool-down:** Easy 200 alternating freestyle and backstroke by 25s.

---

If your swimmers are to take learning each stroke seriously, they need opportunities to compete in each. Try to plan some of your meets so most athletes can swim their less-developed strokes. Again, this is a swimming "strategy" you can use to good effect; you'll appreciate the depth your team has developed when you get to the championship meet.

Emphasizing all the strokes is also important in developing relay teams, because the medley relay requires one strong swimmer in each stroke. The lack of a butterfly or a breaststroke swimmer will doom even the best of the other three relay legs to a mediocre finish.

Some coaches follow a philosophy that "all swimmers are IM swimmers." The individual medley, considered the decathlon of swimming, requires endurance as well as technical expertise and stroke-specific speed. The IM event itself, whether 100, 200, or 400 yards, is a specialty, requiring a transition from using one set of muscles to using an entirely different set. The turns from one stroke to another also require balance and technique. You need to develop some sets to specifically teach these transitions from one stroke to another.

---

### Sample Training Set

12 × 75 on 1:15. Rotate strokes: 1st—25 butterfly, 25 backstroke, 25 breaststroke; 2nd—25 backstroke, 25 breaststroke, 25 freestyle; 3rd—25 breaststroke, 25 freestyle, 25 butterfly; 4th—25 freestyle, 25 butterfly, 25 backstroke. Have swimmers repeat this cycle three times.

---

When training and teaching specialty strokes (a swimmer's stroke of preference), remember to break each stroke apart at times to have swimmers do some kick sets, some pull sets, and some swimming sets in that stroke. Individuals will be strong in their specialty strokes to the degree that you have demanded the strokes be swum in practice.

To give swimmers a training balance, design some sets that let the swimmers choose their strokes and others where you designate the stroke to be swum.

## Recognizing and Developing Individual Talents

Each swimmer is uniquely constructed in body build and physiology. It's important that you learn to recognize and respect these differences.

## Different Body Types and Strengths

The differences among your swimmers will show up in various ways. Some athletes may be unable to swim the stroke exactly the way you teach it, but they will make minor adaptations to accommodate their individual body types and strengths (see Figure 8.1). For example, because of her size Janet Evans swims freestyle with a straight arm recovery to get a longer stroke distance. While not a "perfect" stroke, it is an effective adaptation.

**Figure 8.1** Swimmers will make minor stroke adaptations to accommodate their individual body types and strengths.

There is a degree of art to knowing what is a disregard for the basic principles of a stroke and what is an individual variation based on a swimmer's intuitive kinesthetic understanding of how to get more power and speed. Swimming is a never-ending learning process: As we begin, skills are crude, but as we practice, they continually improve. The "ideal" stroke is what you teach, but along the way you'll need to allow for adaptations or customizations of strokes to meet the uniqueness of individual swimmers.

## Endurance vs. Sprint Swimmers

A second common difference among swimmers is physiological makeup. Some young people will have marked endurance characteristics, while others will show explosive potential; they will tend to express a natural preference for one or the other. Typically, the endurance athlete will benefit most from endurance speed training and competing in endurance events, while the explosive athlete will gravitate toward the shorter events.

This difference is related to slow- and fast-twitch muscle fibers. (We have only one explosive event in swimming, the 50 free.)

You can make some educated guesses about your athletes' muscular nature by observing them carefully. The "sprint-oriented" athletes will do everything quickly when they are motivated. Time some 12-1/2 yard sprints on land; seeing who runs fastest for the short distance will give a clue as to who your explosive athletes may be.

Few novice teams or leagues compete in longer distance events, which places the endurance athlete at a competitive disadvantage. These athletes need to be directed toward programs that will enhance their natural ability and provided meets that allow them to express their talent. The coach can be very constructive in reassuring endurance athletes that there is an important place for them in swimming (though it may not be in a novice program).

The explosive athletes also need some special care. Fed a steady diet of short, explosive work, they will improve to a limited degree, but they also need aerobic work to succeed. Encouraging them to do this work can be a task! Sprinters also need substantial rest between sets. With novice teams, discipline problems sometimes result when swimmers have too much rest time in a workout. Your best bet is to offer just a little high-rest work during the week and spend most of your time teaching technique (which acts a lot like active rest time anyway).

Most athletes you coach will not be so strongly categorized in terms of muscle physiology; most will possess a good mixture of muscle fibers and will respond nicely to a mixture of training. You simply must be aware of the two extreme types and make sure your team program accommodates such swimmers.

## Building the Team Aspects of Swimming

No swimmer could ever do alone what is required to train effectively. Each swimmer needs a coach, teammates, and support mechanisms to succeed. Although athletes race alone in our sport, they don't prepare alone. Your swimmers will rely on their teammates and on you to provide the training stimulus that improves performance.

## Encouraging "Good Words"

Encourage "good words" at practice. Remind swimmers to compliment teammates on good sets, good swims, and good attitudes. "Catching someone doing something right" should be a key phrase in your practices, which is where improvement happens. By expressing and encouraging a "can-do" attitude, you will go a long way toward improving your team's performance. Teammates should recognize that they are the primary support mechanism for each other.

**Figure 8.2** Team cheers help develop team harmony and excitement.

---

**"Good Words"**

"Nice set, Michael—stay with it!"

"Get right behind me, Megan; I'll help pull you through this."

"Troy, you did a set almost this hard last week; c'mon, hang in there."

"Becca, I've never seen you work this hard— Keep it up!"

"Tony, you haven't complained once about the cold water today. I think you're getting tough!"

---

## Team Building

Team cheers, a time-honored tradition in swimming, are a perfect way to develop team harmony and excitement (see Figure 8.2). This is also an area where any athlete, regardless of swimming skill, can shine as a leader. Enthusiasm is the key to being a team cheerleader. Team banners, swimsuits, shirts, towels, and so on are visible and highly valued symbols of team unity. But an emphasis on "things" shouldn't be the priority in team building. Unity can also be fostered by allowing older swimmers to help out younger ones and through team events like potluck meals, overnight meets, and community service activities.

Team and individual goal setting and activities like motivational clinics with speakers or videos and buddy workouts with continually changing buddies are valuable team-building experiences. Here are a few examples of simple but useful goals for a novice swim group:

- "Last meet we had four disqualifications. This week let's make sure we stay legal in every race."
- "We should make sure every swimmer who gets on the blocks in this meet hears a team cheer with their name in it."
- "This week let's have every swimmer in a team swim cap!"

The team aspects of swimming can be highly supportive of the individual. As the coach of a novice team, you need to monitor team chemistry carefully to make sure that a small group of talented swimmers doesn't receive most of the support at the expense of other athletes. Team support must mean support for *everyone*.

## Teaching Athletes How to Race in the Pool

There are at least four segments to every race, and you'll improve your team greatly by working on each one:

- The start
- Midpool swimming
- The turns
- The finish

## Start Practice

You'll want to hold start practice fairly often. Good starts are important to racing success, and practicing them is usually a popular activity. Use as close a sound as possible to the actual starting signal. Take time to review procedures for the start, then do repetition practice, perhaps pairing athletes up to critique each other on specific points you assign them to look for. Meanwhile, you supervise the entire group.

Another possibility is to race the starts competitively to a predesignated spot along the pool deck. Relay practice can be fun, exciting, and a good physical workout. As always when working with dives, safety comes first.

## Midpool Swimmming

At the novice level, working on racing tactics such as pacing and negative splits is generally not appropriate. Your emphasis should be on teaching athletes to swim the strokes smoothly, correctly, and with minimum resistance and maximum power. One point you may want to teach is bilateral breathing (breathing every third armstroke) so swimmers can see easily to both sides when they race.

## Turn Practice

To practice turns, line the team up in the shallow end of the pool and have them repetition-train their turns: As soon as the swimmer ahead returns to the front of the line, the next swimmer sprints to the wall to turn. All athletes should wait quietly and standing up so they can benefit from your feedback to each athlete. To end each short turn practice session, have swimmers race the turn from a designated starting spot and back to that spot, through the turn. In this part of the exercise, let them yell their hardest to support their teammates.

## Finish Practice

Good finishes are important to successful race tactics. The athlete must concentrate on reaching the wall at full speed and with full extension of the arms.

Swimmers should attend to these elements in their finishes:

• Start judging the wall about 10 yards from the end and then adjust the stroke.

• Finish at full extension.

• Fingertip-touch the wall.

• Extend and get on the side in the freestyle and the backstroke.

• Learn to "lunge" to the wall in the breaststroke and butterfly.

• Accelerate the kick to help finish fast.

• Keep the head down to help the body extend.

Encourage good race finishes at the end of every practice swim, but practice some specific finish time once or twice a week. Have swimmers line up in lanes in the shallow end and sprint to the finish wall, one at a time. Critique each finish for the group.

## Key Points to Success

Building your swim team happens as a result of what you do in practice. Competition is simply an opportunity to measure your work and your swimmers' improvement.

Your novice season will be so short that there is no point in considering the concept of taper (a decrease in training volume designed to increase rest and store energy for a championship). It takes 6 to 8 weeks for the chemical changes to occur that would require a taper, and most novice seasons do not last that long.

Be aware that the technical orientation of swimming requires much more preparation time than other sports for athletes to enjoy their participation. In soccer, for example, any child can derive some fun from simply running after the ball and kicking it in the correct direction. But no child will enjoy trying to swim a 50 butterfly or breaststroke unless the youngster has been properly prepared to do so.

Provide opportunities for young swimmers to appreciate the complexity of the sport. This is a challenging goal, yet perhaps one of the most important that the novice coach can strive to achieve.

## Vision Provider

Take seriously your role as the "vision provider." You are responsible for letting your swimmers know how much more there is in their sport. Here are some ways to help provide vision.

### Set Up a Bulletin Board

Use half of a bulletin board for team information, posting the day's practice session and so on. Use the other half to educate swimmers (see Figure 8.3). Post articles from swimming publications about other teams, other young swimmers, other coaches, other meets. Let your athletes read about high school and college swimming, the U.S. national championships, and the Olympics. Call attention to the heroes in our sport.

**Figure 8.3** Use a bulletin board to educate and motivate your swimmers.

## Invite Guest Speakers

Inviting local guests to talk briefly to your team can provide variety as well as education. Topics could include the following:

- **Nutrition:** Many community hospitals have speakers available.

- **Self-talk:** We all are affected by our internal dialogue; high school or college staff like guidance counselors may be able to address this topic.

- **Strength training:** Almost every community has a gym; a person knowledgeable about youth sports training could make an enlightening 30-minute presentation.

- **Swimming gear and training devices:** Recruit an experienced coach from a high school or club team to talk about swimming equipment, suits, and other training devices that can help improve performance.

- **Parent education:** Arrange for an experienced coach to talk with parents about the experience of swimming and what is important. This reinforcement of your values and teaching can be invaluable.

- **Motivation:** Sit your team down yourself and tell stories that you know (or can learn) about famous swimmers and famous races. Strive to be a good, exciting, stimulating storyteller.

- **Videos:** Videos are indispensable teaching tools that can provide excellent visual models for athletes to copy.

As you can see, there are many ways you can add to your coaching and teaching to improve the swimming experience for young athletes. As you become more entranced by your own coaching experience, you have many resources to turn to for improvement. Use the resources listed elsewhere in this book to keep yourself current, technically prepared, and well educated about your sport. If you do, your coaching career will provide you with great personal satisfaction, whether you have a part-time volunteer position or a paid coaching job. You have a crucial part to play in each young athlete's development as a person and as a swimmer.

# Appendix

This plan for a novice swim team is based on 1 hour of practice each weekday (Monday through Friday) and Saturday swim meets.

The number of minutes per activity is listed in parentheses.

| | Monday | Tuesday | Wednesday | Thursday | Friday | Saturday |
|---|---|---|---|---|---|---|
| **WEEK 1** | Discussion of team operation, responsibility, rules (20)<br>Warm-up, with explanation of how to do a daily 5-min warm-up (10)<br>Explanation of pace clock use (10)<br>Simple set of 10 × 25 using pace clock (10)<br>Kickboard relay (10) | Warm-up (5)<br>Discussion of swimming rules for each stroke (15)<br>Short freestyle set (10)<br>Demonstration of freestyle turns (5)<br>Freestyle turn practice (15)<br>Short relay, start in the water (10) | Warm-up (5)<br>Discussion of start rules (10)<br>Demonstration of start (5)<br>Start practice in deep water (15)<br>Short non-freestyle set (15)<br>Freestyle teaching (10) | Warm-up (5)<br>Freestyle set (15)<br>Demonstration of forward start (5)<br>Start practice from end of pool, no blocks (10)<br>Backstroke teaching (5)<br>Backstroke set (10)<br>Kickboard relay (10) | Warm-up (5)<br>Breaststroke teaching (10)<br>Breaststroke set (10)<br>Start practice, blocks (10)<br>Freestyle set (15)<br>Backstroke set, sprinting (5)<br>Cool-down swim (5) | MEET |
| **WEEK 2** | Warm-up (5)<br>Breaststroke set (10)<br>Backstroke set (10)<br>Freestyle set (10)<br>Backstroke turn teaching (15)<br>Freestyle relay from blocks (10) | Warm-up (5)<br>Butterfly teaching (10)<br>Turn practice, back and free (10)<br>Butterfly set (5)<br>Start practice (30) | Warm-up (5)<br>Freestyle set (15)<br>Discussion of finishing well (5)<br>Finish practice (10)<br>Backstroke set (15)<br>Medley relay (10) | Warm-up (5)<br>Discussion of IM turns (10)<br>IM turn practice (10)<br>Freestyle set (15)<br>Butterfly set (5)<br>Kickboard races (15) | Warm-up (5)<br>Freestyle starts (10)<br>Freestyle relays (10)<br>Backstroke starts (10)<br>Backstroke teaching (10)<br>Backstroke set (10)<br>Cool-down (5) | MEET |
| **WEEK 3** | Warm-up (5)<br>Breaststroke teaching (10)<br>Breaststroke set (10)<br>Breaststroke start teaching (10)<br>Start practice (5)<br>Breaststroke turns (5)<br>Turn practice (5)<br>Breaststroke relay (10) | Warm-up (5)<br>Butterfly teaching (10)<br>Butterfly set (10)<br>Butterfly start teaching (5)<br>Butterfly start practice (5)<br>Butterfly turn teaching (5)<br>Butterfly turn practice (5)<br>Butterfly relay (15) | Warm-up (5)<br>Backstroke teaching (10)<br>Backstroke set (10)<br>Backstroke start teaching (5)<br>Backstroke start practice (5)<br>Backstroke turn teaching (5)<br>Backstroke turn practice (5)<br>Backstroke relay (15) | Warm-up (5)<br>Freestyle work, same pattern as Wednesday | Warm-up (5)<br>IM set (10)<br>IM turn practice (10)<br>IM transition set (10)<br>IM relay (15)<br>Cool-down (10) | MEET |
| **WEEK 4** | Warm-up (10)<br>IM set (15)<br>Freestyle start teaching (5)<br>Freestyle start practice (10)<br>Freestyle set from dive (15)<br>Freestyle relay (5) | Warm-up (5)<br>IM set (15)<br>Backstroke turn practice (10)<br>Breaststroke turn practice (10)<br>Free set, longer swims (15)<br>Cool-down (5) | Video day (view strokes, starts, and turns; relax with popcorn and party day) | Warm-up (5)<br>Endurance swim (15)<br>IM turn practice (15)<br>Freestyle sprints (10)<br>Discussion of meet (15) | Stroke review: drill each stroke 15 minutes each | MEET |

| | Monday | Tuesday | Wednesday | Thursday | Friday | Saturday |
|---|---|---|---|---|---|---|
| **WEEK 5** | Warm-up (10)<br>Butterfly set (10)<br>Backstroke turn practice (10)<br>Breaststroke set (10)<br>Freestyle start practice (10)<br>Freestyle relays (10) | Relays: swims, kicks, special strokes, etc.; fun day | Warm-up (10)<br>Backstroke set (15)<br>Breaststroke turns (10)<br>Breaststroke set (10)<br>Freestyle sprints (10)<br>Kickboard relays (5) | Warm-up (5)<br>Freestyle teaching drills (15)<br>Freestyle long swim (20)<br>Butterfly short sprints (10)<br>Butterfly teaching drills (10) | Warm-up (5)<br>IM turn drills (15)<br>Relay start teaching (10)<br>Relay start practice (15)<br>Choice sprint set and cool-down on own (15) | MEET |
| **WEEK 6** | Warm-up (10)<br>Swim (15)<br>Backstroke start work (5)<br>Freestyle finish practice (10)<br>Breaststroke sprints (10)<br>Butterfly relay (10) | Warm-up (10)<br>Breaststroke technique (10)<br>Breaststroke set (10)<br>Backstroke turn work (10)<br>IM relays (20) | Warm-up (5)<br>Sprint kicking, all strokes (10)<br>Discussion of championship meet (15)<br>Backstroke stroke work (10)<br>Freestyle stroke work (10)<br>Freestyle relays (10) | Warm-up (5)<br>Review all starts and turns (20)<br>Discuss meet procedures (35) | Warm-up (15)<br>Short freestyle set (10)<br>Backstroke technique set (10)<br>Breaststroke technique set (10)<br>Butterfly technique set (5)<br>Plan team cheers (10) | MEET |
| **WEEK 7** | Warm-up (10)<br>Review IM turns (10)<br>IM set (20)<br>Review freestyle turns (10)<br>Freestyle set (5)<br>Kick relay (5) | Warm-up (5)<br>Review all finishes (10)<br>IM set (10)<br>Review back turns (10)<br>Back set (15)<br>IM relay (10) | Review videotapes (of Olympic Games or similar) | Warm-up (10)<br>Swim (15)<br>Review breaststroke and butterfly turns (10)<br>Freestyle sprints (10)<br>IM relay (15) | Warm-up (5)<br>Backstroke set (10)<br>Breaststroke teaching set (10)<br>Short butterfly sprint set (5)<br>Freestyle relays (20)<br>Discussion of meet (10) | MEET |
| **WEEK 8** | Review championship meet information (15)<br>Warm-up (10)<br>Freestyle set (10)<br>Freestyle starts (15)<br>Backstroke set (5)<br>Backstroke starts (5) | Warm-up (5)<br>Breaststroke set (10)<br>Breaststroke starts (10)<br>Butterfly set (10)<br>Butterfly starts (10)<br>Review relay starts (15) | Warm-up (5)<br>Sprints, all four strokes (10)<br>Turns, all four strokes (20)<br>Finishes, all four strokes (10)<br>Meet reminders (15) | Warm-up (5)<br>Practice team cheers (10)<br>Choice of stroke sprints (15)<br>Swim (15)<br>Note improvements of all swimmers in 15-minute swims over season (15) | Warm-up (10)<br>Practice finishes (10)<br>Practice relay starts (10)<br>Discussion of meet (30) | CHAMPIONSHIP MEET |

# *Swimming and Coaching Books*

## Coaching Young Athletes

**Rainer Martens, PhD, Robert W. Christina, PhD, John S. Harvey, Jr., MD, and Brian J. Sharkey, PhD**

1981 • Paper • 224 pp
Item BMAR0024 • ISBN 0-931250-24-2
**$18.00 ($24.95 Canadian)**

This guide introduces and explains the basics of coaching, such as coaching philosophy, psychology, pedagogy, physiology, sports medicine, parent management, and sport law. Lots of exercises, examples, discussion topics, illustrations, and checklists make learning interesting and enjoyable.

## Coaching Swimming Successfully

**Dick Hannula**

*Foreword by Skip Kenney*

1995 • Paper • 200 pp
Item PHAN0492 • ISBN 0-87322-492-2
**$18.95 ($26.50 Canadian)**

This book shares the secrets to becoming a great coach. It provides important details for teaching perfect technique in the crawl, backstroke, breaststroke, and butterfly and shares the five essential ingredients of a winning formula.

## Swimming

*Steps to Success*

**David G. Thomas**

1989 • Paper • 192 pp
Item PTHO0309 • ISBN 0-88011-309-X
**$14.95 ($19.95 Canadian)**

## Teaching Swimming

*Steps to Success*

*David G. Thomas*

1989 • Paper • 168 pp
Item PTHO0310 • ISBN 0-88011-310-3
**$19.95 ($27.95 Canadian)**

The unique progression of skills in these books will help swimmers get started quickly, make steady progress, practice in performance contexts, and correct problems as they develop. Coaches and instructors need both the participant guide and the instructor guide. While the participant book presents the skills, the instructor guide shows how to teach those skills most effectively.

## Advanced Swimming

*Steps to Success*

**David G. Thomas**

1990 • Paper • 168 pp • Item PTHO0389
ISBN 0-88011-389-8 • $15.95 ($21.50 Canadian)

This second-level continuation of *Swimming: Steps to Success* features 18 steps designed to help swimmers review and improve the crawl and breast strokes, learn the new competitive back and butterfly strokes, and master competitive strokes and turns.

## ASEP *SportCoach* Training Programs

The American Sport Education Program (ASEP) provides two *SportCoach* courses for educating volunteer youth coaches. The **Rookie Coaches Course** is for first-year coaches with little or no formal coaching experience. This *Rookie Coaches Swimming Guide* serves as a text for the course. The **Coaching Young Athletes Course** serves second- or third-year coaches who want more in-depth information on coaching principles. Both *SportCoach* courses help coaches establish an athlete-centered philosophy, communicate to and motivate young athletes, teach sport skills, plan effective practices, manage risk, and promote safety. ASEP encourages youth sport coaches to complete both the **Rookie Coaches Course** and the **Coaching Young Athletes Course**.

In addition to these two *SportCoach* courses currently available, ASEP is developing a series of sport-specific skills and drills videos designed to show you how to teach and communicate basic skill and drill information to young athletes. Call the ASEP National Center toll-free at 1-800-747-5698 for more information on any of ASEP's educational programs. Let ASEP help you expand your coaching skills and knowledge. Your athletes will be glad you did!

**Human Kinetics**

*Prices subject to change.*

Place your order using the appropriate telephone number/address shown in the front of this book, or **call TOLL-FREE in the U.S.**
**1 800 747-4457.**